Maureen Lamb grew up on the outskirts of London during the Second World War, moving to Exeter to experience the Baedeker raids on that city. Teaching geography and history took her to Kent, to Canada and then to Yorkshire and Lancashire. She had always been interested in writing and has published text books on geography and essays on local history. Now in her nineties, she writes to encourage people to look forward to old age which may even be the happiest and most rewarding time of life.

To my husband, Donald, and my children, Malcolm, Sheena and Moira, who gave me the time and space to write this book.

Maureen Lamb

The Older the Ginger, the Hotter the Spice

Austin Macauley Publishers™
LONDON • CAMBRIDGE • NEW YORK • SHARJAH

Copyright © Maureen Lamb (2021)

The right of Maureen Lamb to be identified as author of this work has been asserted by the author in accordance with section 77 and 78 of the Copyright, Designs and Patents Act 1988.

All rights reserved. No part of this publication may be reproduced, stored in a retrieval system, or transmitted in any form or by any means, electronic, mechanical, photocopying, recording, or otherwise, without the prior permission of the publishers.

Any person who commits any unauthorised act in relation to this publication may be liable to criminal prosecution and civil claims for damages.

A CIP catalogue record for this title is available from the British Library.

ISBN 9781398405998 (Paperback)
ISBN 9781398406001 (ePub e-book)

www.austinmacauley.com

First Published (2021)
Austin Macauley Publishers Ltd
25 Canada Square
Canary Wharf
London
E14 5LQ

Apology
The graph on page 211
has wandered there by accident

Introduction

What does it feel like to be old? As any academic will tell you, it all depends on what you mean by 'old.' At 60, I thought I would be old at 70. Now at 80-nine, I still do not feel old. I have met 90- and 100-year-olds who would not admit to be really old. As the Duke of Edinburgh once said, "It is not so much the age but being able to survive the celebrations."

Age is not a number; it is a state of mind and it is not marked by a sudden recognisable change in physical strength or social outlook and certainly not by a change in personality. These banners that flutter today on roundabouts announcing 'Bill is 50' are all nonsense. In some countries such as Thailand, they do not even feel the need to celebrate a person's birthday. Shakespeare's seven ages of man are popular stereotypes and are cartoon characters. We may, from time to time, say, "I feel as old as Methuselah today," or, "I feel as young as a bird," but what we really experience is not age as a countable number. We experience what it feels like to be me. Ask any 70-year-old, and they will say, "I still feel 30 on a good day."

The problem is, being old is so very different from people's perception of it.

A nurse who had worked for many years in old people's homes, once described to me what other people called 'her old dears.'

"For me," she said, "I do not see an old lady rocking backwards and forwards in her chair. I see a young girl, outgoing and full of life, chatting with friends, excited about her wedding, revelling in her children, the lively friend of her grandchildren. And when she talks to me about her life, she is still that same person, still with a desire to engage with people, still able to listen to me and comfort me in my troubles. Nothing has changed, except the way other people look at her as she sits in her chair."

So much of our impression of people in our society and perhaps in most western societies depends on outward appearance. Perhaps carers should not be asking, "What can I do for you?" but, "What can you do for us?"

To see Granny D with her wrinkled face and her spine held in place with a metal shield, you would never imagine that in her 80-ninth year she would set out to walk across America, from California to Washington, giving speeches in town halls along the way. She did it in protest against the money spent on election campaigns. It took her a whole year and she suffered the extreme heat of the Arizona Desert, and snow and ice while crossing the Appalachians, but she made it.

As Abraham Lincoln remarked, "It is not the years in your life that count, it is the life in your years."

Lincoln's life was cut short at the age of 56 by assassination, but his words apply equally to those who live to be 80 or 90.

Abraham's advice was sound, but I would go further.

Being old is likely to be the happiest time of your life!

That cannot be true, can it?

We know this is certainly true in Europe and the UK for most people, as a result of an extensive survey of 20-one countries that was done in 2008. People were asked to rate how satisfied they were with their lives on a scale of one to ten. All classes of society were questioned, from the very rich to the very poor and two age groups reported the greatest satisfaction with their lives, those in their teens and those over 50. The least satisfied were those in the 40-50 age group ~~(see graph on page 164)~~

Life begins at 60, despite the pessimism of the 40-year-olds. You really are as old as you feel, not as old as you look.

Why is it that at 60, life begins to look so good? This book is about what I discovered.

Maureen Lamb
February 2016

Chapter 1
How Old Is Old?

Middle age ends and senescence begins the day your descendants outnumber your friends.

Ogden Nash

How old are you? If you are between ten and 70, it is a question you do not expect, or even want to be asked. But outside that age range, people are often pleased to be asked their age, and the old as well as the young are often quite proud of it. Which is odd, really, because it is said, and it is probably true, that most people want to have a long life, but they do not want to be old. Yet, old people often seem to be proud of their age, so it cannot all be bad.

What we do know is that all of us are living longer, and not only in the west but throughout the world, the number of old people as a proportion of the total will increase.

The US census bureau records that life expectation in the USA in 2006 was 77.85 years, but by 2050, it will go up to the mid-80s[1]. In 2005, in the UK the number[2] of those who were of state pension age was only slightly less than the number of 1-15-year-olds. Perhaps for the very first time in the history of man on earth, society will have to face up to the fact that it will have to adjust to the demands of the old. Their impact will be as great as that of the young and of childbearing adults. The balance is changing.

So, when does old age begin?

Bertrand Russell, philosopher, aged 80, memorably said, "This world takes a lot of getting used to and I have only lately begun to feel at home in it."

If a woman can give birth at 63 (Rosanna Dalla Corto, Italy), an ex-president (George W Bush) can make a parachute descent for his 85th birthday and a 98-year-old Sikh (Fauja Singh of East London) can run a marathon, can we call them 'old' without redefining what it means to be old?

Unlike most other stages in life, the beginning of old age is not easily pinned down. It is fairly clear when a baby becomes a child and puberty obviously marks the onset of adolescence. For most, getting married/ partnered and raising a family is the beginning of adulthood, but what marks the onset of old age?

A survey[3] examining 60 societies around the world attempted to discover how each society decided what it was that marked the onset of old age. A very small proportion of them defined it in terms of chronological age as we tend to do in Western Europe and North America. Less than a third thought it had to do with capabilities or physical decline. Many saw it in terms of the social role, of becoming an elder, for instance, or of receiving more than they give in financial and economic terms; that is, they are no longer working. However, perhaps surprisingly, most saw it linked to maturity and spiritual growth.

In the developed world, we have a retirement age, usually of 60 or 65, when there is an assumption you are too old to work anymore. The word 'retirement' itself says much about western society's view of old age. Retirement is the equivalent of 'withdrawal'; withdrawal from an active part in the life of the community. During the 19th and 20th centuries in the west, this represented what actually happened. In the United States in 1960, life expectancy after retirement was just four years and I can remember my father, who worked on the railway, bemoaning the fact that so many of his colleagues died soon after retirement. Those working in uninteresting and uninspiring jobs looked forward eagerly to their retirement, which then lasted but a few short years. It is tempting to believe that withdrawal from the daily grind of paid work, in one sense becoming useless, actually hastened the death of many. In other societies, the old have had a valuable role to play even when they are unable to be part of the economic life of their community.

Old Age in the West

This pattern in the west developed as a result of the industrial revolution. Until then, life had largely revolved around the home, whether it was in farming or in producing goods that were later produced industrially – textiles, iron working, milling, pottery making, joinery – these were all produced domestically in premises attached to the dwelling. It was Richard Arkwright in the 18th century, who, if he did not invent the factory, was certainly the man responsible for the spread of the factory system, that for the first-time tied employees, who were no longer called artisans, to a place at a distance from the home, and to a work regime dominated by the clock. Not only adults, but children as young as six, were divorced from their homes, working six days a week, 12 or more hours a day in an alien environment. In the 20th century, the age of starting work may have gone up and the hours of work reduced but the dominance of the workplace, as opposed to the home, has not decreased. For the last 200 years, the office, as well as the factory, has become the 'hearth' for many people; hence the unexpected emotional effect of suddenly being wrenched from it at 60 or 65.

In the USA in 1935, the Social Security Administration reckoned that only 15% of the population would actually reach the age of 65 but by the 1990s, 80% were living beyond 65 years, very largely as a result of improved health and new opportunities. Most of them could look forward to 20 or even 30 years in so-called retirement. The speed and extent of the change that has come about are staggering and it is worldwide. It is now necessary to redefine the concept of old age and to see what can be learned from the past and from world studies about how we can plan for the elderly in the future.

Gerontological studies in the 1960s[4] and 1970s came up with a number of theories about providing for the aged, which both reflected and justified what was already happening in the USA, South Africa, Australia,

New Zealand and Western Europe. One study[5] proposed a 'disengagement theory', which suggested that segregating the elderly into their own communities was most likely to provide for them a life in which they could find satisfaction. It was feasible because of the new affluence of many and because of the better health enjoyed by people who retired in their 50s and 60s, and who were ready to spend their later days re-living their fondly remembered holidays. As one retirement village in Florida said in its advertising, 'Live your dream! The village is like a permanent vacation…that's what makes it so great.' Many of these residential villages are in holiday vacation areas which offer beautiful locations, as well as the sunshine, such as Florida, Spain, Cyprus, or in the UK in Cornwall and the Cotswolds.

Perhaps the fact that many of these are so-called 'gated villages', serves to emphasise the real purpose of them, which is to offer security and protection from the pressures of modern life by segregating the elderly from the world outside. In one sense, the 'gate' serves not only to keep out the real world but to keep in its inhabitants, providing them with only limited opportunities to mix in any meaningful way with people of all ages. The choice of a retirement village is most often dictated, not by its geographical location – being near to where the individual grew up, worked or where their relatives lived – but where the accommodation and facilities suited the aspirations and the purse of the individual. It is an acceptance of the fact that he or she no longer has an active role to play in the economy, the social life or the politics of the society from which they came. The jury is out on the long-term psychological effect of this segregation.

In those societies in which there has never been a chronological retirement age, there are other ways of viewing old age.

Old Age in the East

There are still a few places where even today, people, from choice, continue to work to a very old age. They remain economically useful to their society. This can be found in Japan, in Okinawa, a string of islands running south from the main islands. Here, even centenarians continue to work in the shops or in the fields.

"She walks a bit slower, and her hearing isn't what it used to be," but Fumi Chinen, just a few months shy of her 100th birthday, hasn't given much thought to retirement.

"I would hate just sitting round the house," Chinen said, during a recent afternoon break from tending her family's small clothing shop in the public market. "I think I'd go senile."[7]

The Japanese have the highest average life expectancy of any country in the world: 86 years for women and 78 years for men. It even higher in Okinawa. There are now 457 people over the age of 100; that is 42 for every 100,000 people. The equivalent figure for the United States is 10.

Researchers have offered a number of explanations for the longevity and the fitness of old people in Okinawa. Their genes undoubtedly play some part and diet seems to be an important factor (in the 20th century, 100,000 Okinawans emigrated to Brazil, adopting the Brazilian diet, rich in meat, and their life span was reduced by 1 7 years); but it is undoubtedly also the result of the way Okinawan society functions. The Okinawans not only live a long life, but it appears they enjoy their old age. Their social network supports them, gives them certain expectations and opportunities, and above all, makes them feel active members of the community. They are even keen on hobbies, with people in their 90s riding mountain bikes or motorcycles, taking long walks, practising karate (which originated from Okinawa) or joining in community tai chi sessions. They seem to have low levels of stress, and depression is almost unknown. They are mutually supportive and have a positive view of life. In such a social environment, it seems there is little need or desire for retirement and no thought of segregation from the community.

In most parts of the world, although the onset of old age is not related to a specific chronological age, it is almost always recognised as a separate stage of life when new roles are ascribed or adopted. This is seldom connected to declining physical or mental ability. A significant landmark maybe the date when you become a grandparent. There is often a change in status when you start to have grandchildren. Where people rely on subsistence agriculture, you will leave the group who are economically productive and take on the new and important role of looking after the very young children, supervising them, feeding them and often preparing food for the whole family when they return home in the evening. In other societies, old age starts when you join the council of elders, becoming an accepted source of knowledge and wisdom.

Even in modern atheistic China with its populous cities and industrial work patterns, the idea that it is the role of the grandparent to look after the grandchildren is taken for granted. A westerner who had a baby boy while living with her husband in Shanghai was frequently asked if she would be sending her son home to be looked after by his grandparents. She tells of her housekeeper, who had somehow avoided the restriction on family size and had had three children. For 20 years, this lady had been working in a factory in Xinjiang Province, 72 hours away from her home in Shanghai, but once her children were old enough, she had sent them to Shanghai to be looked after by her parents.

The historic attitudes of the Chinese towards family as yet remain intact but there are signs that things are changing as they already are in Japan. There, in the 19th century, the Meiji Restoration insisted on bringing back the samurai ideal of a patriarchal family, where it was the duty of the eldest son to care for his parents; and this remained strong throughout the 20th century. In the 21st century, caring for the old in Japan has started to become a problem, because of the ever-increasing number of elderly people. Japan is now the most aged nation with over 20% of the population over 65. A few 'silver seats' on public transport, reserved for the elderly make little sense when 90% of the occupants are all elderly. More of Japan's old people now live on their own and care homes are becoming commonplace. It appears that the consequences of 21st century medical care and the adoption of the 21st century market economy are rapidly overriding the existing culture and fundamental changes have begun to appear.

Why do People Live Longer in Some Societies?

Yet another society claiming to have one of the world's longest average lifespan is a group of Seventh Day Adventists living in Southern California, at Loma Linda, whose religion encourages them to follow a healthy lifestyle and who have a spiritual view of life.

We know then, that in strong and reasonably affluent societies throughout the world, many not only live to a great old age but live to enjoy it. In these societies, spiritual values underpin a culture of social responsibility. The old are integrated into everyday life. This is in contrast to many western societies, which are based on material values and which celebrate freedom and individuality. In the west, many old people appear to be marginalised.

Why should this be so? The precise reasons for it are far from clear. It has been suggested earlier that work patterns created by the industrial revolution may have some bearing on the differences between societies. May it also be the size of the social groupings? Or the effects of urbanisation? Or is it related to spiritual beliefs? All the major world religions, including Christianity, of course, emphasise the duty of the young to care for the old. Are the elderly becoming marginalised because of the increasing proportion of the elderly in the population? Is it caused by affluence? Or is it in fact something even more fundamental; that western values, which raise the importance of the individual above the importance of society? We do not know the answer to this question, but an understanding of why in the west the elderly are marginalised is vital in order to bring about a change in attitude.

Will our experience of living in our old age in the 21st century depend upon what our own society has ordained for us, what our economy dictates or what demographics will demand or can we learn from other cultures and also from our own history how best to plan for the old? No society in the past has had so much accessible research to enable it to shape the world of the future, with its unique problems of ageing. The knowledge now available from anthropological and gerontological studies and the medical advances, which have vastly improved the physical wellbeing of the elderly, open up new horizons for us. Living as I do in a small village in Cumbria, I could not have written this book without the knowledge available to me through the world wide web. Can this knowledge at a societal level, together with examples of the lives of iconic people at an individual level, give us hope that we can all enjoy long and successful ageing?

Chapter 1 Notes

1. US Census Bureau
2. 2005 in the UK 18.7% were of state pension age – 11.2 million out of 60.2 million. See www.statistics.gov.uk
3. Sokolovsky, Jay, 2009, The Cultural Context of Aging, Praeger, London
4. Shenk, Dena, and Achenbaum, W. Andrew, 1994, Changing Perceptions of Aging and the Aged
5. Cumming, E, and Henry, W, 1961, Growing Old: the process of disengagement: New York, Basic Books
6. Associated Press, 7 October 2001
7. Turnbull, Colin, M, 1983, The Human Cycle, Jonathan Cape

Chapter 2
Ageing in Simpler Societies

Far from being useless and unproductive, the old in every society are a vital source of richness and strength.

Colin Turnbull[1]

Our biology tells us that increasing age limits the amount of physical work a person can do. Western civilisation has its roots in classical culture and in Christianity and this has shaped our attitudes towards those who are no longer capable of childbearing or of making an economic contribution to their communities. This was obviously so when most work was physical work on the land, in industry or in the army. With the emphasis on economic return, those who were not physically fit, which included most of the aged, were often seen as a burden. Even more recently in western societies, now that the population of elderly people is growing, even though most of those over 65 are far more fit than their predecessors, as a group they are not valued or considered an asset, except perhaps for their spending power. There is no role assigned to them. In contrast, there were and still are many societies in which the roles of the oldest members are clearly designated, understood, and accepted.

On a blog I came across recently, someone asked, 'Why do old people love telling stories?' In most parts of the world such a question would be incomprehensible. 'Who else can tell us these stories?' would be the comment.

In very many cultures, children grow up knowing that all knowledge of importance comes from old people. This is not only because of their own experience, gained through a long life, but also because of the knowledge they have acquired from their parents and grandparents. It is obvious even to the youngest child. Such conversations are intrinsic to their understanding of the world.

This attitude is not limited to primitive societies, whose people do not read and write, and so they need to pass down their history through word of mouth, nor is it confined to the past. A recent example comes from an island in the Pacific, which, in 2004, suffered the disastrous tsunami that was responsible for killing over 200,000 people in the East Indies, India and Africa. On this island, there were many people on the beach when they saw the sea recede a great distance from the shore, as if something was sucking up the water. This had never before happened in their lifetimes, but they had heard stories from their elders about the way the water disappears from the shore before a huge killer wave strikes. They all dropped everything and ran frantically to higher ground before the oncoming wave moving at 300 miles an hour struck the beach. No one was killed.

Many people still live in small, cohesive social groups – the tribe, the clan or the village – in which the individual is just one cog in the whole. Individuality is not encouraged.

Unlike those in the west, who prize freedom and individuality above all else, these people do not. Their society makes a conscious attempt to make individuals aware of their social responsibility. In threatened societies, this is fundamental to survival. The society is seen as a unit, with each age group having its own unique role to play in sustaining its health, whether it be defending the group against outsiders or providing food and shelter. In such societies, the knowledge and wisdom of the old are often considered of even greater value than the economic and child raising activities of the adults. It safeguards their future.

Storytelling is one of the vital roles played by the old in these societies. There are many others. Colin Turnbull[1], an anthropologist, who spent many years in the second half of the twentieth century living with tribes in Zaire and Tanzania in Africa and amongst the Tibetans in India, believes that much can be learned from them about what they believe the old can bring to their society; "In all societies, old age brings physical and mental defects, weakening powers of body and mind," but he goes on to say that old people have much to offer society because, "Heart and soul are more alive than ever."

Turnbull calls old age the 'anteroom to extinction', and he believes that it gives an old person a special perspective on life. The very closeness of the elderly to nonexistence, like the proximity of a baby to nonexistence, is a source of amazement and perhaps a source of special powers seldom recognised in western societies.

His study of these societies led him to produce a list of ways by which an aged person can contribute to society – through knowledge or wisdom; through example or in his words 'saintliness'; or through mystic power. They contribute either as seers, saints or as witches.

The wisdom and love that grandparents shower upon their grandchildren are a worldwide phenomenon, although in western societies, it may even become a cause for conflict. An Observer headline, 'Are Grannies Rebelling?' reflects such an attitude. The article announces a new website for grandparents (see the 'Ground Rules' on grannynet.co.uk), which suggests the need for a Grandparents Charter because the demands on them for childcare may sometimes be felt as excessive. By contrast, in many tribal societies, the role of the elderly in relieving parents of childcare is part of the contract, which ensures that the elderly will receive care when they are no longer able to look after themselves, although such care may be shared amongst the extended family. That grandparents would create conflict is unthinkable; rather, their role in resolving conflict within and between the generations is clearly set out; it is essential to the smooth running of the society.

It is not just that older people have accumulated a certain amount of wisdom during their lifetime, but the fact that they are set apart in the way they live and because they have limited aspirations, it enables them to have a more balanced view of a problem or a dispute. This is both taken for granted and highly valued.

Perhaps it is not altogether a wild conjecture to believe that when old people are accorded such respect, they respond to expectations, living up to the image that the younger generation ascribes to them and perhaps even living longer than might be expected. In many African communities, it is the tribal elders who still hold power, so that in Kenya in 2008, a Kenyan Nobel Prize winner appeals to the tribal elders of the Kikuyu ethnic group, the Luos, Luhyas and Kalenjins to urge their young warriors to cease their squabbling. Power in our political arena seems to be in the hands of younger and younger people.

Turnbull's category of 'saint' is of people, just ordinary people, who have influence, because of the example they set. This is above all to do with 'being' rather than 'doing.' It could simply be that by the way they appear to live a contented life as an old person, whatever their infirmities or responsibilities, that they inspire others. The word saint is familiar in the religious context, but sainthood is not limited to Tibetan monks, Hindu Sadhus or Christian martyrs, whose lives are devoted entirely to subjugating self and desire to the demands of their religion. Self-denial is at the heart of sainthood, but it can be on a domestic scale, looking after a dying friend, a spouse with dementia or grandchildren bereft of a mother. However, it is not the work involved that denotes saintliness, but the sacrifice.

And saintliness is quite unconnected with the assumption that a person has been saintly throughout their lives. Neither can it be seen as a person who does good deeds or is a source of knowledge. Saintliness is something perceived by others in an elderly person because of what they are. They inspire, but they make no conscious attempt to inspire. Their calm assurance seems to say they have solved the riddle of life, a riddle that you then feel you too may one day be able to solve.

Siddhartha

A novel by Hans Hesse[2]. Hesse was born a Brahmin, a high caste Hindu, with a deep understanding of Hindu philosophy, but eventually he turned to Buddhism. It is a story of a handsome and devout young Brahmin, the pride of his parents because of his learning and religious devotion. But this is not enough for Siddhartha. He left home to become a samana, an ascetic, who wandered the countryside, thin as a skeleton from fasting and with hair and nails that were never cut. But even this did not bring him the understanding he sought. And then he found it, in a beautiful woman. They were married and had a son and he became rich and powerful, but the emptiness of his life eventually made him very depressed. He left his wife and took to gambling. He became even more depressed and contemplated suicide.

Now this would hardly seem to qualify Siddhartha as a saint. He had spent his life endlessly seeking meaning, purpose and happiness, but it is not until towards the latter part of his life that he realises it is not the 'seeking', it is not wanting to become something that will solve his problem; it is just by 'being.' The solution as to how life is to be lived lies within. He becomes a child again, seeing the world anew, in the now, soaking up experience, not trying to direct it. But he does not preach his new discovery. He knows each person has to learn it for himself. It is just through his presence that people draw inspiration.

It is in Hindu and Buddhist societies that developing saintliness is more overtly an aspiration and these religions illustrate more vividly than others that peace in old age comes not so much as a result of leading a good life, but of understanding the inner self. Its message is that peace and joy come not from doing or seeking to understand, but just by living for the now, savouring every moment, good or bad, accepting that you are what you are. It is something that cannot be taught but the saints in our lives provide the inspiration.

This is at the heart of all religions and there is research evidence to show that in the west, people who go to church regularly live longer than others. An outstanding example is a group of people who live in southern California, at Loma Linda. Their average lifespan is greater than anywhere else in the USA or anywhere else in the world, apart from Okinawa and Ovodda in Sardinia. The explanation seems to be that they are mostly Seventh Day Adventists. Their religion encourages them to follow a healthy lifestyle, and church attendance, bible study and developing a spiritual view of life are at the core of their day-to-day living.

The idea of a witch, someone with mystic powers, posed by Turnbull is the most difficult to grasp for 21st century western society, but if we look round our own communities, we may recognise what he means by witches, although their role is seldom appreciated and they are more often scorned, persecuted or laughed at. In primitive societies, witches may be feared, mistrusted or left alone, but they are seldom harmed. A story that comes from India, from Varanasi, towards the end of the 19th century, is almost incomprehensible to us but it has within it an idea that is certainly familiar to our children. I remember as a ten-year-old, deciding that one small bungalow on our road, which was surrounded by trees and undergrowth, was lived in by a witch. I persuaded my sister that we must always run past that house for fear she would exert her power over us.

At the festival of the Balua Fair, an old woman of Varanasi sat by the Ganges for five days, shaking her head, but saying nothing. This strange behaviour had a profound influence on those around her. Was she in touch with the spirits? Whatever it was, it was an influence that led to rioting and death. Sometimes, old people may have an influence over others that is neither logical nor rational, but powerful nevertheless.

The Old Woman of Varnassi

The year was 1865 and it was coming close to the time of the Balua Fair, a festival that marked the beginning of the Hindu solar year. It seems that an old woman had been sitting by the river shaking her head. She sat there for five days, speaking to no one, taking no food, just shaking, shaking her head. No one interfered with her, but the sight of her had a profound effect. Was she in touch with the spirits? Clearly, she had some strange power.

Just at that time, two boatmen, who earned their living by fishing in the Ganges said they had brought a letter from the God Dalai, which ordered the boatmen to stop fishing and to become devotees of the God. This caused consternation among the fishermen. The strange command had been strengthened by the sight of the woman continually shaking her head. That gave the message its power. To them, she was no longer a useless and stupid old woman shaking her head, but being close to death, they believed some special knowledge spoke through her silence. The outcome, unfortunately, led to death and rioting, largely because the ruling British stepped in as they entirely misunderstood what was going on.

Based on his studies, Colin Turnbull suggests that really old people, because of their closeness to death and through their lives, have acquired knowledge of a kind denied to younger people, have powers which may be for good or for evil. In many societies, if they do become a force for evil, or just an annoyance, people will fear them but not blame them, because it is recognised that they are not in control. It is taken for granted that these people are completely unaware of the power they are exerting. They will be allowed to dress in strange ways and express unacceptable opinions; but they also provide useful scapegoats against whom no action will be taken because their lack of response renders them harmless.

In contrast to modern western society, which provides them with medical diagnoses, and in the past just 'put them away', this attitude is of very positive value for elderly witches. Turnbull says that because it ensures they are left alone, and given deference, they are assured of a measure of security. It also has a positive value for society, giving the elderly a place. It resets the balance, reminding those engaged in constant activity, that those who are just 'there' have a valid perspective, and that they have important lessons to teach about the mystery of existence.

In societies outside the west, the old have a variety of essential roles to play, whether it be as grandparents, as witches, saints or wise men (and women); and most societies cannot imagine how they would exist deprived of their elderly. However, when the elderly become a burden, because of their health or because of the scarcity of resources, where the future of the tribe or group may be threatened by their very existence, everyone grows up with the understanding that there is a time to take leave of life. This may be eased for the individual by the tribe's particular belief in the afterlife, but it should also be understood in light of the fact that the concept of the self as an isolated, independent individual is not universal.

Even in the society of Western Europe, until the advent of the Enlightenment, the dead body of the individual was not at all important. Bodies were incarcerated in charnel houses and buried in communal graves. Except amongst the nobility, it was not until the 18th and 19th centuries that tombstones became popular.

Think of society as a sieve full of small pebbles, all different in colour and shape and composition but roughly the same size. As the sieve is shaken, they rub against each other and are partly changed, but in essence, they remain the same. Those at the bottom eventually fall out, lost forever and new ones replace them at the top. This is our view of life in our society. We pass through life knocked around and shaped by others but retaining our identity. Death is final and so it is horrifying for many to contemplate and solace has to be found in some form of belief about an afterlife. Compare this to societies which are more like trees which have leaves, each of which is unique but each of which is part of a whole that makes up the beauty and the life of the tree. As the leaves fall off and die, they decompose and form the food for the next generation of leaves. For them, death is the beginning of new life. To die is not a sacrifice, but an offering.

Suicide or assisted death has been common throughout the world's history, especially in places where life is under stress. In many communities, death is not an extraordinary event, but part of life, at any age. With such a mindset, the idea of euthanasia or suicide is no longer horrific. In the Arctic, some Eskimo tribes had a tradition of ceremonial assisted death, by shooting or hanging, or sometimes the old were expected to commit ritual suicide when left alone in their igloo. The Tiwi, a Pacific Island tribe, would leave a really aged person, who no longer understood what was going on because of their infirmities and who was a danger to themselves and others, in a hole dug in the forest, with just their head above ground. Returning a couple of days later, they would be dead and no one was responsible. Turnbull reports that amongst the tribes he visited, it was not unusual for an elderly frail person to go out into the bush and not to return. They were often never found.

Assisted Suicide Among the Yuit

In the past, the Yuit, a group of people living in the harsh conditions of the St Lawrence island off the coast of Northern Siberia, ritualised planned death at the hands of the clan. Their livelihood depended on fish and sea mammals, such as seals, but there were times of extreme hunger. When an elderly man indicated he wished to die because he was becoming a burden on the group, he was dressed in a special funeral robe and ceremonially killed. It might be by hanging or by stabbing or shooting. The public nature of the event and its ritual avoided the problem we have with assisted suicide, because it could only occur with the consent of the whole clan and not just at the behest of the immediate family.

How horrific all this seems to the western mind! We want to skim over the words, relieving them of their meaning. Perhaps we should try to view this through the eyes of the so-called primitive, if he were brought to see the plight of some of our elderly people, rescued by doctors from death, but now, lying in a hospital bed, hooked up to all kinds of lifesaving apparatus. The patient may be wishing hourly that death would take them, but they are kept alive because the hospital and their nearest and dearest think it is the right thing to do. Of course, in the Hippocratic Oath, doctors swear to 'care for the sick'; but it also says, 'If it is given to me to save a life, all thanks. But it may also be within my power to take a life.'

Even in the recent past, it was not unknown for a doctor to allow a patient to die, or not to strive to keep alive, at all costs, a baby born with a horrific disability. The oath goes on to add, 'this awesome responsibility must be faced with great humbleness and awareness of my own frailty. Above all, I must not play at God.'

It is a quandary which can only lead to endless debate. On the other hand, today, our Christian (and insurance orientated) society, exerts a pressure that doctors cannot ignore. It is interesting to remember that the origin of the oath is not from the Christian moral code but from Classical Greece.

For those who have become weak and decrepit and who are no longer able to look after themselves and who become a burden to those around them, some kind of provision has to be made. In industrial societies, this is still an unresolved problem. In more primitive societies, the actions taken to forsake, abandon or even to kill people can seem to us to be indescribably cruel. In Victorian times, the word used to describe primitive societies was 'barbarian', and indeed many of the practices of native peoples are quite abhorrent but they were often the only solution they could find in such extreme circumstances.

In non-industrial societies, the capable elderly not only continue to have an important role to play in childminding, cooking, counselling, advising, conducting ceremonies and so on, but they are usually well looked after. But how like us they really are!

Koka, aged 80, a member of the Ju/'hoansi (pronounced Juntwasi) tribe in Southern Africa comments, "Old people have always complained: it is an old thing. Even if a child did everything for them, they would still complain."

The researcher says that the Ju/'hoansi complain all the time. "They are cranky, funny, loud," but she adds that they live in a moral universe of high caregiving standards, in which everyone is obligated to help everyone else.

When an old lady called Chwa was very ill with a fever, she was cared for by a neighbour and a co-wife, who, "Poured water on me. I slept in their arms…my heart craved for bush food and the women collected it for me."[7]

When her helpers were asked why they thought of doing that, one replied, "What is there to think about? You see an old person. She is your person. She can't walk. She can't do it for herself, so you do it."

Society may have developed certain norms of behaviour, but individuals will adapt their behaviour to whatever they perceive is urgently needed by another individual. And pose dilemmas to which we all have to find an answer.

As the next chapter will show, it was in western society that until very recently, growing old was more to be feared than to be desired.

"As we age, having seen many cycles of birth and death, there is a detachment and a wisdom that grows within us."

Chapter 2 Notes

1. Colin M Turnbull The Human Cycle 1983
2. Herman Hess, Siddhartha, Picador 1998, London
3. No Aging in India: Alzheimer's, The Bad Family, and Other Modern Things (Paperback) Lawrence Cohen 1998 (Varanasi)
4. Hippocratic Oath A widely used modern version of the traditional oath was penned in 1964 by Dr. Louis Lasagna, Dean of the School of Medicine at Tufts University:
5. Yuit Accessmylibrary.com Assisted Suicide: reference 10 (see Source material)
6. YUIT – Charles Hughes, 1996 Encyclopaedia of World Cultures www.encyclopedia.com
7. Jack Kornfield, quoted for 10/11 February in the book called Buddhist Offering 365 Days, Thames and Hudson/ Stewart, Tabori and Chang, New York Danielle and Oliver Föllmi

Chapter 3
The Aged in Western Society

A Caring Society?
My neighbour is very well looked after, judging by the number of milk bottles on her doorstep

A News Clip

Some work done recently by evolutionary anthropologist Robin Dunbar[1] suggests that the human brain is only capable of having meaningful relationships with about 150 other people. This is approximately the size of many tribal communities, in which the health and survival of the group depend upon roles being ascribed to all age groups because every member has a vital part to play. What is good for the community has to be good for individuals within the community. Individual actions or a show of independence may endanger the very stability and even the existence of the group and everyone is acutely aware of that. Change is a threat; the elders hold the wisdom that has ensured the existence of the tribe for generations. This gives the older members of the tribe great authority and ensures that in most of these societies the old people are respected and cared for irrespective of their physical condition.

To discover the origins of the west's attitude towards old age you have to go back 3,000 years. In the Middle East and in the Eastern Mediterranean, the settled communities based on agriculture that eventually emerged from the hunting and gathering groups created a population explosion. The increased density of population allowed the growth of towns and of centrally controlled states. In 3,500 BC, the first cities developed in the fertile crescent around the Tigris and the Euphrates, present-day Iraq. In such a populous state, it was no longer possible for everyone to know everyone else. As a result, these early nation states – Persia, Minoa, Egypt, Greece and then Rome started to develop centralised authorities with laws handed down from the king or head of state. They developed centralised religions, which gave the monarch his moral authority. Social customs were no longer kept in place by the mutual consent of the whole tribe, but writing enabled laws to be written down and some kind of police or military force had to be engaged to enforce the laws.

The development of a comprehensive body of literature in classical time gives us a first-hand glimpse of the place of elderly in society. Although there are many sources of such information, it has to be remembered that these were all written by the wealthy educated elite and entirely by men. Their perspective is limited.

Even before that, the Old Testament makes clear that it is the moral duty of children to look after aged parents. In the Jewish text, adopted later by Christians, God commanded, "Honour thy father and thy mother that thy days shall be long in the land," a dictum I was brought up with.

In classical times, there are many allusions to the duty of offspring towards their ageing parents. The care of the elderly was never seen as the duty of the state, except insofar as laws were made to enforce the duty of the family. In Athens, in the fifth and sixth centuries BC, a statute declared that children owed a duty to their parents because of the time and energy the parents spent in caring for them when they were young. The strong sanctions imposed by law included deprivation of citizen rights, a harsh sentence. There was a caveat, however: if the offspring could show that they had not been well cared for; or if a daughter had been put to prostitution to raise money for the family, for instance; or if the child was a bastard, the son or daughter no longer had any duty of care towards their elderly parents.

The downside to this appears to have been the fact that even when families took their duty seriously, the elderly became totally dependent on their children and lost all power. They sometimes became the objects of ridicule because of their frailties. In Aristophanes, 'The Wasps', the aged father complains he is treated like a child. The son Bdelykleon says of him, "I'll support him, providing everything that is suitable for an old man: gruel to lick up, a soft, thick cloak, a goatskin mantle. a whore to massage his prick and his loins." [2] There is little reverence here.

It appears that while a man was reasonably fit in body and mind, he retained his position in society. After that, as Tim Parkin comments (p 46), "Old people...felt themselves prisoners in their own homes."

Regarding women, we know little. As the wealthy of Greece and Rome relied for domestic chores on slaves, it seems unlikely that grandmothers had an important role to play with, regard to raising grandchildren. It also seems that because men married late in life, aged 30 or more, and women married much earlier and because of high mortality and low fertility rates, three-generational households were not the norm. It has been calculated that aged 20, fewer than one in 100 individuals would have had a surviving grandfather.

For the wealthy in Greece and Rome, the important thing was to remain healthy into old age. Cicero's 'De Senectute',[3] written in the first century BC, has a very modern ring. It seems to have been written to confute those who were complaining about old age, but there is no mention of reliance on filial care or of assistance or moral direction from the state. The emphasis is entirely on what the individual can do about it – 'Old men of self-control, who are neither churlish nor ungracious, find old age endurable; while on the other hand, perversity and an unkindly disposition render irksome every period of life.'

It is entirely up to you! Cicero prescribes healthy eating; exercise of the body to keep fit; exercising the mind to maintain the memory; seeking knowledge and learning new skills; keeping busy; enjoying a social life with the young, as well as with contemporaries; and not regretting the loss of those faculties that made life pleasurable when younger – 'Each stage of existence has been allotted its own appropriate quality; so that the weakness of childhood, the impetuosity of youth, the seriousness of middle life, the maturity of old age — each bears some of Nature's fruit, which must be garnered in its own season.'

During the Middle Ages in Western Europe, the proportion of people living to beyond 60 was relatively small. War took many young men and many women died in childbirth. The Black Death and the plagues that followed, which may have killed well over half the population of Europe, attacked the young and not the old, so if you did survive to be 60, you would be likely to live to be 70, 80 or even 90. If you knew that there was only a one in 20 chance that you would live to be that age, you would hardly spend much time thinking about it or preparing for it. If you did, you probably hoped it would not happen. It echoes something the Greek satirist Lucien said nearly 2000 years before, at the funeral of his son; that it was better to die young so you would not have to grow old and look like your father, 'with bald head, face wrinkled, back bent, knees trembling.' By dying young, 'he will not be scorned in old age, nor will the sight of him offend the young.'4 Much later, it was Montaign who said, 'To die of age is a rare, singular and extraordinary death, and so much less natural than others.' 5

In the Middle Ages in Europe, old people of all classes were more often reviled than revered. Old women especially were thought to have evil powers, having passed through the menopause, it was thought that venomous humours now remained inside the body. Religious and didactic texts usually represented all the virtues as young women, while all the vices – sloth, pride, treachery, flattery, gluttony, anger and avarice – would be represented by old women. Sloth, for instance, was represented as an 'ugly, hairy, dirty and stinking old woman'6. An old woman was a hag, a crone or a witch, even.

Old men were equally marginalised and denigrated. Though relieved of military duties, trial by battle and payment of some taxes, men over the age of 60 were classed with invalids, women, the very poor and foreigners.

Whatever their class, they no longer held any power, political or otherwise. Power resided with the young and the middle-aged, among officials of the church, as well as for high offices of state. The elderly were accorded no advantage because of their age and wisdom. It seems that only in the Venetian Republic was age a qualification for election to high office. It was that of the Doge, and that may have been partly because they wanted to be sure that no one would have too long a reign!

If you were poor and old, the suffering could be extreme. When you could no longer work, if you had no children – or if your children rejected you because of their own poverty – begging was your only option. There is a medieval story about one old man who was reluctantly given a home by his son. In his bedroom, he kept a locked chest, which he told everyone contained his legacy. This persuaded his son to treat him well. When the old man died, they grabbed the key from his body and opened the chest. In it was a club with a note, 'This is what a son inherits if he looks after his father in old age, reluctantly.' 7

The people of the middle ages were clearly appalled by the physical appearance of old age and because of the lack of medical knowledge, the extent of the suffering it brought. But although medieval society was not democratic, unlike Greece, and although unlike Greece it had adopted a Jewish/Christian philosophy, it had in common with classical times the idea that it was the individual himself who had to accept the responsibility for his old age and that it was not the duty of society to carve out a specific role for him. The classical and Christian demand that it was the duty of children to take care of and support the elderly was not necessarily interpreted as a command to provide physical help. Some monasteries offered a home to those who could afford it and some of the wealthy built almshouses for the elderly poor, often as way of securing their own place in heaven, but in general, the church emphasised that by recognising the importance of the soul, individuals should be able to come to terms with the suffering and indignities of old age. The church was more concerned with the afterlife than the present, with the soul rather than the body. Ideally, it was recommended that old age should be spent in prayer and meditation, preparing for the afterlife. The elderly were relegated to the margins of society, left to themselves to suffer old age and prepare for salvation. They not only had to bear the burdens of infirmity and loss of mental faculties, but they were virtually outcasts. In marked contrast to many supposedly more primitive cultures, society no longer had any use for them, unless they were particularly outstanding individuals with strong characters, who kept their faculties to the end. Was this due to the size of a country like England or France and the density of its population, with an autocratic government at its centre, as opposed to small self-governing units such as a group or tribe? It could be argued, however, that most villages in England were small and had a strong sense of community, similar to that of a tribe. The big difference was that power did not reside with the villagers, acting in common assent, but with the lord of the manor and ultimately with the law of the land. It was an autocratic society rather than a cooperative one.

One other important factor, which was typical of western Europe and perhaps especially typical of Britain, was the ease of and desire for mobility. The rivers, the sea and a system of roads, bequeathed by the Romans, that were entirely suitable for horses, meant that moving around the country and moving goods around the country was commonplace. England was a trading nation and wool in its raw state or woven up into cloth was regularly moved long distances. Kendal in what might be considered the remote north of the country sent weekly consignments of cloth to London or to Newcastle. People engaged in this trade often married and settled in towns far from their birthplace and far from their parents.

I live in a cottage that has been the dwelling of millers who had worked in the adjacent water mill for over 400 years. In 1586, it was lived in by a widow, Elizabeth Mealbank, but her son Edmund, who was a wool packman, lived many miles away in Stockton. I was able to discover this because of an indenture which recorded the fact that Edmund bought the property for his mother. The indenture states, 'to sell unto the said Edmunde Mealbank, his heirs and assigns forever the said message and tenement... and all the singular barns, stables, houses, buildings, orchards, gardens, yards, lands, meadows, pastures, woods, underwoods, closes, grounds, commons, commons of pasture, passages, easements... emoluments, liberties... lodges and other hereditaments whatsoever... being at Broad Raine Killington.' It appears to have been a considerable property, but lawyers at that time were none too precise in their descriptions often using the same formula over and over again!

Elizabeth, his mother, died a year later and Edward came to live at Broad Raine. It was a familiar pattern at that time, with the son going away to work and returning to the family home much later in life, too late to look after his parents.

Come the 18th and 19th centuries and the industrial revolution, the movement of people from their villages into the towns or the emigration of people abroad became even more commonplace. It was the younger generation that would move away to find work, marry and raise a family, and their parents who were left behind had to look after themselves. Ever since then the dispersion of families has increased and now in the 21st century, grown-up children living many miles from their parents still find it difficult to care for elderly parents, despite improvements in communication. Every day, I meet people stressed out because they travel 100s of miles on a regular basis to give support infirm parents. It tears into their lives. Over the last two and a half centuries, the state or charitable societies started to make some provision for the elderly, especially the elderly poor, but it has always been inadequate. By the end of the 19th century, although 55% of the elderly were able to support themselves and just another 5% relied exclusively on their relatives, the remainder, some 40%, relied on charity or the state 8.

The Poor Law Report of 1834 had a very pessimistic view of the situation.

"The duty of supporting parents…in old age is so strongly enforced by our natural feelings that it is often well performed, even among savages and almost always so in a nation deserving the name of civilised. We believe that England is the only European country in which it is neglected."9

Throughout Western Europe, the answer to this problem was the building of workhouses and similar institutions, which served impoverished young people as well as the elderly poor. These were mainly run by the state but also by the church and other charities.

The workhouses were dreaded. They were huge institutions with harsh rules and relentless work. Men were separated from their wives, children from parents. The regime was draconian. The workhouse was to be avoided at all costs. Begging was a preferable option. In some countries, beggars were tolerated and giving to beggars was a charitable act that earned merit. In England begging became illegal under the Vagrancy Act of 1824. Although the law was not always enforced, begging needed courage and it invited harassment. Things have changed little. A beggar in 20th century California holding up a placard, sums it up: 'WiLL Take Verbal Abuse for MONEY – God BLESS.' State pensions were never more than a token contribution towards a person's needs for food and shelter.

Those who were old and rich or had a modicum of wealth were nevertheless also marginalised. In Europe in the 17th century, bed and board contracts became popular, by which those too old to look after their affairs were given an apartment or sometimes a property to which they could retreat and meditate in preparation for their demise. In some ways, this was the beginning of the idea of retirement. As they were no longer a useful member of society in the economic sense, society was pleased to put them out of sight, in Turnbull's phrase, in the 'anteroom' to death.

The attitude in the new world appears to have been equally hard hearted in the early 19th century, where independence and the ability to 'plough your own furrow' were the admired and necessary qualities for survival.

"Nothing is more incumbent on the old than to know they shall get out of the way and relinquish to younger successors the honours they can no longer earn, and the duties they can no longer perform," declared Thomas Jefferson.[10]

Thomas Jefferson, though, was not a man prepared to follow his own advice. He was already 72 when he wrote this, and although retired, he spent the next 11 years of his life, writing letters – in one year, writing 1,268 – gardening, taking a two-hour ride in the afternoon and entertaining many, many guests and he worked as an architect improving his neo-classical house at Monticello, building a retreat at Bedford and designing the campus of the University of Virginia, for which university he then chose all the books for the library, designed the curriculum and picked the faculty.

During the late 19th century and most of the 20th century, it was in the realm of politics that age and experience were recognised as valuable. Many politicians in senior positions were old men. By then it was no longer possible for a young man, such as William Pitt the Younger to become Prime Minister at the age of 24. William Gladstone retired aged 66 but he was called back to office five years later and remained in office, on and off, for the next 19 years. The average age of the prime ministers of the 20th century was 58. Only three took office under the age of 50 – Harold Wilson and then the very last two, John Major and Tony Blair, who were in their late 40s. Winston Churchill was brought in to run the country during the Second World War when he was aged 66, the time of retirement for most people. In the 21st century, that seems to be reverting and it is the young who are now in charge in politics.

It would appear that it was mainly in Northern Europe and North America, in contrast to most of the rest of the world, that what to do about people beyond working age, had always been a problem. Margaret Mead's anthropological studies in Indonesia and Samoa in the mid-20th century threw a new light on so-called primitive cultures, but she upset many who had held a superior attitude towards them. Some Americans were not pleased to hear her say, "I have spent most of my life studying the lives of other peoples – faraway peoples – so that Americans might better understand themselves."

Of the UK and the USA, she notes, "Nobody has ever before asked the nuclear family to live all by itself in a box the way we do. With no relatives, no support, we've put it in an impossible situation."

In southern Europe, especially Spain, Italy and Southern France, there had always been a tradition for several generations of a family to live under one roof. In fact, there are few parts of the world where this is not the normal practice. In the Moslem countries of the Middle East and North Africa, among the Hindus and Buddhists in India and South East Asia, and also in China, even after the communist ideology replaced ancestor worship, a household normally consisted of the extended family, though the parents may for part of their working lives, lived away from the ancestral home.

In these cultures, the older generation was assured of a home and food, but it was not necessarily treated with veneration. Perhaps Margaret Mead overstated the case, but she did recognise that in the communities she studied in New Guinea, which she wrote up in her book, 'Sex and Temperament in Three Primitive Societies', the outcomes were very different, depending upon their traditional culture. She noted that a group called the Arapesh, who used no violence in bringing up their children and had pacific attitudes towards one another produced peaceful relationships between generations. By contrast, among the Mundugumor, a rigid upbringing appeared to lead to a warlike attitude towards other tribes and violence within the tribe and the family.

Today, as more countries become industrialised, new patterns of behaviour are emerging and attitudes are changing. In the 20th century, a Chinese civil servant living in the UK, who was partly English, had a slightly different take on the Chinese relationship with grandparents, "We were brought up to respect our grandparents, but this means that grandparents are remote. They get their own way and people run round after them, but they are not their grandchildren's friends."[11]

On the other hand, an Asian man also brought up in England recently commented, "We are taught that our parents are God. Our path to heaven is through them."

In Japan, it appears that despite the very strong tradition that the eldest son should look after his parents, some grandparents are now choosing to go into retirement homes. This trend really only began in the 1990s, but it is escalating particularly now there are fewer young people to look after the growing number that live beyond the age of 70.

In general then, in western society, through from the middle ages to the 21st century, it was clear that once you are too old to work, defined in earlier times by your physical or mental ability, but in more recent times by your age, then you no longer had a role to play in that society. You were waiting for death. Retirement homes are now often referred to by the young as 'God's waiting room.' Up to a point, withdrawal from an active economic life was true both for wage earners and for salaried professionals. Many accept this situation, and as many are relatively wealthy, they create their own society of aged people in retirement villages or they go on round the world cruise liners.

There are many others, however, who do find themselves a new role, a role useful to their community. There have always been volunteers, many in the last 200 years were middle class women, who were not expected to go to work. Today, most of the volunteers are those who have retired, who now wait to greet you at the entrance to a National Trust property, to answer your queries in the Citizen's Advice Bureau or they sit on one of the many charity committees. In some areas, most local magistrates and councillors are retired and many mayors are over 65. If the 'Big Society' idea, which is hardly new, actually leads to the recognition that many retired people are fit and ready for work, perhaps it may become official that the senior citizen (what an ironic term that is!) has a proper, acceptable and even indeed an important role to play in the society of the 21st century.

Many, of course, are no longer fit to help in this way, but a recent television series, *When Teenagers Meet Old Age* (Channel 4) not only showed how much young people were prepared and able to give to help the elderly, but how much even the sick elderly could give in return. A 24-year-old working for a week in a retirement home was asked to care for an elderly man who had had a stroke. It overwhelmed her because her father had died a short while before after having a stroke. To watch a man who talked with his eyes and could squeeze her hand, but who in every other way was an inanimate body overwhelmed her. She had to leave him and weep in the corridor outside. When her week at the home was nearly up, she went back to him to apologise and to explain that it was not his fault that she was so upset, but that he reminded her of her own father. For a moment, there almost seemed a flicker of a smile on his face and he squeezed her hand hard. She thanked him simply and sincerely and admitted afterwards that it had been a healing experience. The old and the frail have so much to give on a level so different from the giving in a commercial world, a giving that is not to be valued in pounds and pence, but in peace of mind and in the ability to accept that life and then death are inevitable. Deprived of speech, he was able to give her what no one else could give her; stillness of heart.

Every individual in the world has a unique contribution to make.

Chapter 3 Notes

1. Robin Dunbar, currently Professor of Evolutionary Anthropology at Oxford, reported in the Observer 14/03/2010
2. Tim Parkin, quoted in The Long History of Old Age p45, Thomas and Hudson, London 2005, Chap 3

3. English translation of the Cato Maior De Senectute by Cicero published in the Loeb Classical Library 1923 to be found on the website: http://penelope.uchicago.edu/Thayer/E/Roman/Texts/Cicero/ Cato_Maior_de_Senectute/text*html
4. Lucien, de Luctu, quoted by Tim Parkin (as above)
5. Michel de Montaign Essays, trans. John Florio (Fayard 1989) bk 1 chap LVII quoted in Long History of Old Age p25 Pat Thane
6. Le Pelerinage de la vie humaine by William de Deguileville (14th century) quoted in the Long History of Old Age page 87.
7. Popular tale quoted in ibid p12
8. C. Booth, The Aged Poor in England and Wales (London, 1984), p339. quoted in ibid, p235
9. (The Poor Law Report of 1834 (repr. London, 1970), p.115)
10. Thomas Jefferson writing in 1815 (Letter to John Vaughan, 1815, quoted in Anthony and Sally Sampson, The Oxford Book of Ages, Oxford 1985, p139.)
11. Mass Observation Archive (University of Sussex), Growing Older Mass observation archive.

Chapter 4

Heroes: How Life's Passions Often Flower in Old Age

Age means nothing to me. I can't get old. I'm working. I was old when I was 21 and out of work. As long as you're working, you stay young. When I'm in front of an audience, all that love and vitality sweeps over me and I forget my age.

1896 to 1996, George Burns.

How many actors, musicians, writers, artists, philosophers never retire? These are all people who have some passion in life; people such as Ralph Vaughan Williams composing major works aged 88, Picasso at 91 still producing great art and Marguerite Patten at 96 still writing cookery books. Then there's Eric Hobshorn, historian, who at the age of 93 published a new book, 'How to Change the World', which shed new light on the global financial crash; and there are so many others.

George Burns, at 98 years old, booked himself in to play at the Palladium in London and Caesar's palace in Las Vegas to celebrate his 100th year. Caesar's Palace was booked out within a fortnight and one might say that it was almost bad luck they did not get to see him. In December 1995, a few weeks before his 100th birthday, he reportedly caught the flu at a Christmas party hosted by Frank Sinatra. By 20th January 1996, his birthday, he was too ill to attend his birthday celebrations. He died 49 days later.

What was it about his life or his lifestyle that made it possible for him to be able to spend an hour on stage, keeping the audience in fits of laughter, aged 98?

When a reporter is interviewing an eccentric old lady or wizened old man who has reached the age of 100 but who is still able to enjoy life and to cope with the stress of being interviewed, he or she can seldom avoid asking the question, "And so, to what do you accredit your great age?"

It is a fatuous question, but journalists know that is what their listeners will expect. Despite the disadvantages of old age, obvious during such an interview, with the interviewee apparently stuck forever in an unfashionable armchair, with wrinkled skin, immobile legs and straggly hair that even the effects man has not been able to arrange neatly, everyone wants to know the secret of old age.

The answers are invariably as useless as the question. An Italian, De Munari, believed the elixir that assured long life was Chianti wine. An American, Dr Ellsworth Wareham, a heart surgeon, believes in pruning trees, mowing the lawn and using the vacuum cleaner, while others ascribe their long life to avoiding exercise. Drink alcohol regularly or avoid alcohol; exercise or become a couch potato; give up smoking or smoke ten cigars a day; aim either to have quiet peaceful life with regular habits and a loving lifelong partner or to a renewed sex life with a new partner at the age of 80. Sir Ralph Vaughan Williams remarried aged 81 and flew for the first time in his life, undertaking a world tour. He went back to writing music with renewed vigour, composing symphonies, instrumental and choral works. He died aged 86, just the day before he was due to supervise a recording by Sir Adrian Boult, of his recently completed Ninth Symphony,

The long life of George Burns defied conventional wisdom. Born the ninth child of a family of 12 in New York's Lower East Side with a father out of work, he hardly had a good start. He smoked, he drank, and although he exercised – he played golf – at a prestigious Los Angeles Golf Club – he didn't take it very seriously. Partnered by Harpo Marx, he said he only went for a laugh. On one occasion, on a very hot day, over 100 degrees Fahrenheit, the two of them turned up without shirts. After playing a round, they were reported to the manager. It seems that the rules stated that shirts had to be worn, and a warning was administered. They were not pleased, but it is always the comic that gets the last laugh. Next day, they arrived in shirts, but having checked the rules very carefully, they wore nothing down below but their underpants. A comic can always beat a bureaucrat. In later years, George's only form of exercise was each morning to walk 15 times around the pool.

George was not even to have the comfort of his beloved wife in old age. Gracie Allan, his wife and stage partner of some 40 years, died when he was 68. His lifelong friend Jack Benny died a few years later. Their deaths were devastating, and he never really recovered from them. Every month, he visited Gracie's tomb in the wall of the Forest Lawn Cemetery and sat on the stone bench, talking to her about the decisions he should make, his successes and his worries; and as always, smoking his cigar.

He smoked between ten and 20 cigars a day for the last 30 years of his life. It started when he was 14 years old. He was already ambitious to make his name in the world as an entertainer. By that time, he had tried dancing, trick roller skating, singing and comedy acts. At an early age, he realised that image was everything. A cigar spoke of success.

Despite the cigars, he enjoyed good health for most of his life. He once said, "If I had taken my doctor's advice to stop smoking, I would not have been alive to go to his funeral!"

In his 70s, he started visiting his doctor more often than he wanted to admit, and at 78, he had a triple bypass operation. He was said to be, at that time, the oldest person ever to have undergone such an operation. Perhaps if he had not been in California with some of the best surgeons in the world, and if by that time, he had not become a very rich man, the outcome might have been very different. He lived another 22 years!

When George was asked the secret of his long life, he said he would have to say, "It's avoiding worry, stress and tension," and if you didn't ask him, he assured us that he would still have to say it.

Yet, his life was packed with action and excitement. He had a radio or TV series running almost continuously for many years, from 1933 to 1950 in radio, before transferring to television; he appeared in 43 films, the last ten of them after he was 80, and he wrote ten books.

In order to live to a great age, having the right genes is a help. Having long-lived parents, aunts and uncles is a good prognosis, but George Burns was much nearer the truth when he said he had a passion for work. It does not ensure longevity but without some kind of passion for life, there is no raison d'etre.

The passion for work and more especially the need for an audience is particularly strong among entertainers and the more famous they become the greater their need for more and more acclaim, more and more engagements. It is part of their personality that perhaps they start out with, but that they certainly develop over the years, as success comes their way.

Benny Hill, who became a television star, whose popularity lasted over four decades, caused controversy from time to time, mainly from feminists who accused him of exploiting sex in his shows. The final showdown came when his *Hills Angels* show was cancelled by the head of Entertainment of Thames Television, because, he said, audience figures were going down.

Benny was totally devastated, and a colleague commented, "He started to die from there..." and what followed was a self-inflicted decline in health. He died five years later, in 1992 aged 68. He was not to know that the day he died; he received a new contract from Central Independent Television for a new series.

There were many reasons why George Burns managed to surmount the inevitable enforced 'rests' experienced by most entertainers; he was able to adapt. As a young man, he was offered a contract to go out on the road for 36 weeks to do a ballroom dance act with a young lady, Hannah Siegal. His father forbade it, because of the infamy of travelling alone with a woman to whom you were not married. For

George, the solution was easy. He married the young lady and when the tour was finished three months later, he divorced her.

When he met up with Gracie Allen, they started off with a double act, but George quickly realised that it was Gracie, not himself, who was getting the laughs, so he altered the routine. George continued to write the jokes, but Gracie was allowed to put them over while George took the part of the straight man. It was an instant success. Constant adaptation of the Burns and Allen Show was the key to their long career. When their radio show grew stale in the 30s, they moved to situation comedy, and in the 50s, they adapted to television. When Gracie died, he changed again eventually becoming at 80, an 'amorous senior citizen.' He won an Oscar – the oldest to do so at that time – for his performance in the Sunshine Boys as a faded vaudeville artist.

At 98, Irving Fein (his manager) said of him, "I would say that…he is the highest-earning person of his age in the world. Nobody at 98 is earning what he makes. There are old people with huge incomes, but it's from clipping coupons and stock dividends. But George is actually out there in the field, earning it as an actor."

The long active life of George Burns surely had some connection with his continued success in front of an audience.

An interesting contrast in lifestyle is the octogenarian entertainer Bruce Forsyth, who has the physical ability of a man half his age. After a long career in show business, he comperes *Strictly Come Dancing* and proves to have almost as much energy as those taking part in the programme. Married for the third time, his present wife is the ex-world beauty Queen, Wilnelia Merced. He met her in 1980, when she was a fellow judge on the Miss World Beauty Competition. At the time of their marriage, she was 23 and Bruce was 55. He has often used young and beautiful girls in his shows and his second wife, Anthea Redfern, was a co-presenter.

A Channel 4 documentary2 followed him daily for several months, and it revealed his punishing exercise regime, which included push-ups and 25 'twirls'! He is equally rigid about his diet, having porridge every morning, with cinnamon and a small number of blueberries placed on top an equal distance apart. He insists on washing his own socks and shirt and is superstitious about the colour green. Although he clearly believes that his rigid attention to diet and exercise is responsible for his lengthy career, and may certainly account in part for his fitness, it is tempting to think that his relationships with his younger wife and young colleagues, as well as with his audiences, have played a significant part in giving him a purpose and a joy in life. And why not?

Entertainers, especially live entertainers, are a special case. Their next contract is not just a food ticket; it is their promise of a supply of the oxygen that will keep them alive. Without the applause of an audience, they are like a car without petrol; they are like a balloon that loses its air; their reason to exist disappears. Writers, artists, musicians need an audience too, but they are less reliant on the immediacy of the applause from a dedicated public. Their work can, up to a point, be satisfying simply for the pleasure of creation, but even a diarist, I guess, has always a secret desire that his or her writing should be discovered, even if it is after their death. Creative people may have a message for the rest of us, but they are less concerned than entertainers to hear for themselves our response.

Grandma Moses started painting when she was 70 years old and by the time she died, aged 101, she had produced 3,600 canvasses. Although she achieved fame internationally and even had a commemorative stamp issued in her honour, she had started painting entirely for her own pleasure. She had been a housewife, bearing ten children, only five of whom survived, but her passion had been embroidery and quilting. It is said she turned to painting because arthritis in her fingers made working with a needle difficult.

In classical times, many philosophers and academics (as we would call them) appeared to have been long lived. Pythagoras probably lived to be at least 90, although some accounts have him living to the age of 117 years. The Seven Wise Men of Greece all died aged between 70 and 100, and Plato, who lived from 427 to 347 BC was 80 when he died. Tim Parkin in The History of Old Age[3], suggests that, "Philosophers are almost by definition old men."

We have examples from our own times. In 1952, Bertrand Russell, when he turned 80, wrote, 'My last ten years, according to the scriptures, ought to have consisted of labour and sorrow, but in fact, I have had less of both than in most of the previous decades. The world takes a lot of getting used to, and I have only lately begun to feel more or less at home in it.'

He was primarily a mathematician and a philosopher, but he had always been interested in politics. He received the Nobel Prize for Literature for his championship of the humanitarian ideal and his was a voice that was listened to. Three days before he died in 1970, aged 97, he had issued a statement condemning Israeli aggression in the Middle East, and the day after his death, it was read out in Cairo at a conference of parliamentarians. His passion for politics had spurred him on to the end.

Most of these are extraordinary people, not because of their long-lived lives, but because they had remarkable talents and made an extraordinary contribution to our society, in entertainment, in music, in art or in writing or academic research. As role models, they are hardly appropriate for us ordinary mortals, but their motivation is common to all humanity and their long-lived lives depended upon that and not on their fame or their outstanding gifts. Their lives had purpose and usually it was that purpose and not society's acclaim that contributed to their longevity.

A much less talented person in the sense that she was not an academic or an artist, but a woman who led a fairly unexciting life working in the office of a shoe factory in the USA, was 'Granny D', as she became known. She had her name officially changed to Doris Granny D Haddock at the age of 96. She exhibited a passion that developed in a remarkable way in her 80s that surely contributed to an active life that lasted until after her 100th birthday.

Doris stayed at home to raise two children during the years of the Great Depression, and then she went out to work, retiring when she was 62. Ten more years of her life were given over to caring for her husband, who developed Alzheimer's disease. She and her husband had been active politically, campaigning to prevent experimentation with the hydrogen bomb in Alaska. Living in New Hampshire for most of her life, in her retirement she involved herself in community affairs, but from none of this would you have predicted what came next. I doubt if she would ever have expected to find herself, at the age of 90, standing up in court after being arrested, and declaring:

"Your Honor, to the business at hand: the old woman who stands before you was arrested for reading the Declaration of Independence in America's Capitol Building. I did not raise my voice to do so and I blocked no hall. But if it is a crime to read the Declaration of Independence in our great hall, then I am guilty."

It was not for this isolated act of benign revolution that she will be remembered, but for a remarkable physical feat: that of walking across America, from coast to coast, from Los Angeles to Washington, a distance of 3,200 miles. She did this, at the age of 89, despite suffering emphysema and arthritis, having bad feet and wearing a metal back plate to support her spine. In the burning heat of the Arizona desert, burning was literally what she suffered on her back. Crossing the Appalachian's snow was quite a different hazard, and for part of the distance, she resorted to skis. The journey took 14 months, and she walked an average of ten miles a day, often stopping off at small halls to give a speech to local people. For the most part, she followed the Interstate Highways, which were not built for pedestrians and at times her chief worry was the thunderous approach of the giant transport vehicles that zoomed past her.

Why at that age would such a woman set off on such a demanding and dangerous journey, wearing out four pairs of sneakers in the attempt? Saving endangered species? Raising money for starving Africans? Working for cancer care? She, in fact, raised no money on the journey, and it was only made possible because of the generosity of the people she met, who each night gave her hospitality and a bed to sleep in. Her goals were entirely political.

The book she wrote about her journey, 'Granny D: Walking Across America in My 90th Year', had the subtitle, 'Never Too Old to Raise a Little Hell.' She felt that she needed to raise hell about the cost of elections in America, costs that had escalated as a result of 'soft donations' towards election campaigns by big business. Speaking about the presidential race, she said that the amount of money being thrown about 'was obscene.' In order to run for office, she declared, "A poor man has to sell his soul, or he has to be a multi-millionaire."[4]

For the next ten years of her life, she campaigned tirelessly, even running for the Senate in 2004, when just before the elections the Democratic candidate for New Hampshire dropped out. After 16 weeks campaigning, she managed to poll 34% of the vote, despite her age (I guess some would not want to elect to office a 94-year-old) and despite it being a strongly republican seat.

She was not without a sense of humour. Tackled on one occasion about gay marriage, a very sensitive subject in the US at that time, and a pitfall for any aspiring politician, she replied, "I'm for love. I don't think the government belongs in my bedroom. I don't want them there. Not that anything's happening there these days!"

Her passion seemed to sweep aside her health problems and it surely lengthened her life. The passion was undeniable. She said, "When you fully dedicate yourself to a good mission, the floodgates of heaven open up for you."

If you believe in heaven, it appears that the gates of heaven were held open for her for an unexpectedly long time.

But there is an interesting footnote. It appears that the idea of walking across America did not come about at first because she wanted to publicise a cause. In 1994, she had lost her husband as well as her best friend. She was depressed. Like George Burns, she had a choice. To give up on life or to build on their memory. She told her son she wanted to do something worthy of them and toyed with the idea of walking across America, a hazardous, as well as a costly enterprise, in every way. Her son suggested that to do this she needed a purpose, a worthy cause. Taking up one of the political issues which had motivated herself and her husband for many years, she embarked on a new career; she became the country's spokesperson for returning to true democracy in America.

Her friend and co-author Dennis Burke said in his eulogy to her, "The important thing Doris Haddock would have you remember was that she was no more special than you, and that you have the identical power and the responsibility to make a difference in the community and the world."

Looking through the lives of these people, it appears that love – a long loving relationship, the support of a loved one or even the memory of deeply loved partner – is one of the ingredients in their recipe for long life.

It is not, however, true for all. For Sarah, Daisy Bates and May Savidge, in the next chapter, it was an eccentric passion not a loving relationship that kept them alive and active into old age.

Chapter 4 Notes

1. Rolph Harris interviewed for the BBC Arena programme, broadcast on 28/03/11 on BBC 2
2. Channel 4 documentary, *Living with Brucie* 13.07/10
3. Parkin, Tim, (Thane, Pat, Editor) (2005) 'The History of Old Age' Thames and Hudson Ltd; London
4. Haddock, Doris, (2001), Granny D: Never Too Old to Raise a Little Hell, Random House, London

Chapter 5
Eccentricity

A civilised society is one which tolerates eccentricity to the point of doubtful sanity.

Robert Frost

Eccentric old ladies on Harleys I can deal with. (Harley Davison motorbikes)

Alison Larkin

It's OK to be eccentric if you are rich; otherwise you are just crazy.

Yvon Chouinard[1]

Eccentric people are not all old, but a degree of eccentricity is surely the prerogative of old age. And it is a cause for rejoicing. Somehow, the shackles of conventional society seem to loosen up. They do not entirely disappear, but neither conformity to current fashion nor criticism by the younger generation is any longer a major constraint on behaviour.

Is this the result of the realisation that conformity no longer matters, because ambition is no longer a driving force, or is it because being older, and surely wiser, the opinions of those who have not experienced old age carry no weight? Whatever the reason, I have met many people who no longer feel it is a crime to put on a cardigan inside out. Why bother! By contrast, others continue to backcomb their hair or wear a cravat long after these styles have been abandoned by the majority.

Sarah (not her real name and places are fictional) is an elderly lady, whom I came to know fairly well and who is considered to be a local character, by some the local eccentric. She is short and dumpy – a God-given shape she has learned to live with – and she is likely to be wearing a bright red woolly hat, or perhaps a lavender baseball cap with a matching tote bag. She makes regular purchases of matching hats and shopping bags at the local supermarket. Her hair, streaked with grey, escapes in wisps from under her hat. If you fell into conversation with her on a park bench, which would happen quite easily because she has an engaging and pleasant way of talking, you would soon forget your first impressions. Although born in a working-class area of Liverpool, she speaks with an attractive nondescript accent. Who knows why she adopted that.

She has no close friends. No one ever visits her. She lives in a small stone cottage. The windows are rotten for want of paint over many years. The straight hung net curtains, grey and unwashed, ensure that no visitor can see what is going on inside. To make doubly sure, there are bushes growing over the windows. A large yew tree overhangs almost all of the small front garden which you enter by lifting up the makeshift loop that holds the gate closed. The birds are well cared for with strings of nuts and fat hung from the yew and replenished very regularly.

The neighbours are very kind, and they offer to help her, but it is not long before she finds a reason for rejecting them – they are too inquisitive – they have ulterior motives. Who knows how many times she has been let down in her life, so that although she is an outgoing and sociable person, she trusts no one.

Now in her seventies, despite her age and arthritis, she is still as chirrupy as the birds she looks after so well. What gives her life motivation? She is reasonably fit, despite her arthritis, and seldom seems depressed. Like many eccentrics, her life is dominated by a strict routine and if you ask her to join you for a meal, she nearly always explains she cannot fit it in because she has so much to do. She goes shopping regularly, but I cannot imagine housework is a priority. She often buys clothes and she carefully alters them to fit. Her arms and legs are unusually short, so they always have to be cut down. Apart from watching TV, at home she sits on the phone, hoping for a call from one of her children who live miles away and seldom visit her.

But what really fills her life and her thoughts is historic research. She has not had an academic career but finding out about the past fascinates her. She knows more about the history of local houses than those who live in them and has filled notebook after notebook with her discoveries from the county archives. She has produced a few small booklets on the history of local villages, on sale for tourists. More recently, it has been family history that has consumed her with passion, and she spends hours on the computer trying to discover the story of her own family. I often wondered if this obsession with the past was her attempt to fill a gaping hole in her own history, an attempt to give herself an identity.

She is a survivor, a person to respect, a person worth getting to know, but not someone that the world that mainly judges by appearances, is ever likely to understand. To them, she is an eccentric but she has learned to make the best of what she has and gives pleasure to those who have got to know her.

Sarah's life is not untypical of many, who, in the 21st century in Britain, live alone and happily to a ripe old age. To the world, in general, they may appear eccentric, but what the world thinks does not bother them. They do not want sympathy, just acceptance.

I first came to hear of Daisy May Bates in the late 1940s, when during my first teaching post at a Secondary Modern School, I found myself teaching geography to a very reluctant group of 15-year-olds. The school leaving age had been raised to 15 and none of the children had expected to be still at school or wanted to be. Engaging their attention was not easy, but geography, unfettered by a national curriculum and broadly interpreted as man and his environment, could venture into many interesting areas of knowledge. The culture of primitive societies was one of those. I came across 'Passing of the Aborigines' 2 by Daisy Bates and my notes, recently revisited, came completely as a surprise. They contained details of Australian aboriginal stories and customs, all of which I had completely forgotten. What I had remembered, but of which there was no mention, were details of the woman herself.

Every aspect of Daisy's life was unconventional. She appears to have been married numerous times, and although her husbands did not die, she was never ever divorced. Her departure from Ireland, where she was born, to Australia at the age of 18, was the result of a scandal while she was working as a governess, which involved a young man's suicide. Later, she was bitterly maligned for suggesting that the Aborigines may have supported cannibalism.

Several biographers have tried to untangle the details of her life but have always been dogged by her own version of events, which was often more fiction than fact. Why, having married Jack Bates in February 1885, was she apparently married on June 10 in the same year to Ernest C Baghole at St. Stephen's, near Sidney – a man who then disappears from the scene? She had one child, by Jack Bates, Arnold Hamilton Bates, but spent little time with him and in later years he refused to resume contact with his mother.

What I remembered about Daisy, however, was her dedication to the Aborigines, whom she lived with almost up to the day she died. I remembered their admiration and worship of her so that eventually she became a feature in their mythology. She did this without conceding anything of her own culture in the many years she spent with them in their encampments. In the unbearably hot and waterless deserts of the Australian outback, she stuck rigidly to the late Victorian dress code, described in her own words as, "a neat white blouse, stuff collar and ribbon tie, a dark skirt and coat, stout and serviceable, trim shows and neat black stockings, a sailor hat and a flyveil, and for my excursions to the camps, always a dustcoat and a sunshade."

"Throughout my life, I have adhered to the simple but exact dictates of fashion as I left it, when Victoria was Queen. Not until I was in meticulous order, would I emerge from my tent, dressed for the day."

I wondered at the time about the washing! Then I remembered something my grandmother had told me about living in the late 19th century. Clean aprons and caps were a must, but the dark coloured dresses and skirts were apparently seldom ever washed if you were working class or even middle class. Cleanliness was next to godliness but only if other people could see it.

Her morals, with regard to her sex life, may have been questionable but her rigid code for the conduct of daily life, even in the desert was not.

"In order to prevent the untidiness that goes to mind and soul if neglected, I have my travelling glass straight before me on my table. I've never yet sat down untidy to any meal tho' I have not even a native visitor. Tired, exhausted with heat and failing health though I may be, I look at myself about to sit down untidily and I am up and repairing the damage."

Daisy's work with the Aborigines began when she was 36. She undertook an arduous journey with Jack Bates and her son on a droving trip, from Broome in the north of Western Australia to Perth in the south, a distance that took six months, riding in the saddle over a distance of nearly 4000 kilometres and that was the end of family life. She spent the rest of her life, almost 50 years, living with and studying aboriginal culture and writing about it.

Her output was prodigious, writing millions of words. Her articles, books and reports have achieved what she set out to achieve, a record of a dying culture. She saw the disappearance of the Australian Aborigine as inevitable. She learned some of their many languages and dialects, recorded their myths and legends, detailed their way of life and perhaps unsurprisingly became a defender of Aboriginal women against the depredations of white men. Although often contentious, her work was recognised in Australian academic circles, as well as by the British Government and she was awarded a CBE.

By this time, her youthful aspirations to be a socialite were replaced by a solitary life in the desert; her pursuit of lovers, replaced by a love of the Aboriginal race.

"My meals and meditations in the silence and sunlight, the small joys and tiny events of my solitary walks, have been more to me than the voices of the multitude, and the ever-open book of Nature has taught me more of wisdom than is compassed in the libraries of men."

By the time she was 71, she moved to Adelaide for a short while, working as a journalist for the Advertiser and received $4 a week from the government to put her papers in order; but it was not enough to live on in a city. So she returned to the outback, living in a tent near Ooldea (in South Australia on the edge of the Nullabor plain, a desert wilderness), continuing to write and to research until she was 86, only moving back to Adelaide because of illness for the last six years of her life.

Daisy Bates' passion was not just to understand the Aborigines but to make the world aware of the sadness of the loss of this relic of a 40,000-year-old stone age culture, a loss caused entirely by the criminal actions of Europeans, bringing disease, loss of territory, modern technology – the gun and the railway – and an alien culture. Although raised as a Roman Catholic but Protestant when it suited her, she felt that to try to change their beliefs would remove from them the foundation of their existence. To suggest that their beliefs that stretched back for thousands of years should be superseded by a foreign religion was an unforgivable violation of these people at a time when their culture was nearing its end.

Daisy Bates had bought property to see her through her retirement but eccentric to the end, by the time of her death, she had spent all the money she had on the welfare of the Aborigines. Most of her retirement was spent in a tent. Was it her need to finish her work that kept her alive for so long?

Psychologists generally agree that the early years are vitally important in shaping the way a person deals with life and the effects are long lasting. Like Janet, Daisy's early life was marked by tragedy. Daisy's mother died of tuberculosis when Daisy was three years old. Her father remarried and died a couple of years later on the way to America. The effect of that on a young child must have been quite traumatic and perhaps explains her inability to establish long-term relationships and her preference for independence and a life of isolation. Nevertheless, she established a 50-year relationship with a dying race and found a cause that she was worth her efforts, that was worth living for.

Daisy Bates exhibited a degree of dedication, determination and an apparent disregard of what most other people thought of her, that was quite exceptional. It is really only in recent years that the value of her work been fully appreciated. Her papers are now held in the National Library of Australia.

Many a genius has been seen as eccentric often because of their obsession with collecting. It was this collection of information, this insatiable curiosity for facts written, calculated or discovered by experiment that has led to scientific progress, from the detailed observation of the stars by Galileo, to the counting of worms in a patch of ground examined and carefully noted down by Darwin as a boy.

The obsession with collecting, often marked in the elderly, is more mundane and has less obvious value. Its motivation may be very different. It may simply be the difficulty of throwing things out – a gift from a half-forgotten friend, a present brought back from Burnham on Sea, a powder puff bought by an ex-boyfriend, a Valentine card or an airline ticket to the Seychelles. After you are dead, these will be thrown in the bin without a thought, but just for now, they stay in the drawer or in the old file. On the other hand, it may be a job only half done, a collection of photos that one day will be put into an album, with names and dates, if you can still remember them, or a half-knitted jumper, a half-finished table lamp. There are things that 'might come in handy' sometime, like the plastic bags or the rubber bands that you can never find when you want them, and when you do, they have perished and are useless. Then there are the really precious things like the tapes you made of your cute five and six-year-old children singing, 'Mary had a Little Lamb'; you threw away the tape recorder but you just cannot throw away the tapes.

There are some people of course who do not have this problem. They have always been ruthless throughout their lives clearing out old stuff. Nearing the end of their lives, they do not want to leave other people the job of disposing of their rubbish. They want to be remembered as tidy and organised and that taken to extremes can be seen as eccentric. Does it matter? Of course, if you believe it matters, it matters. That is the kind of person you are. If you don't believe it matters, then you will believe that after you are dead it will matter even less. Most of us, of course, are in between, so we worry about all our 'stuff', but we still cannot bring ourselves to throw most of it away.

I remember one elderly couple who both died within a short time of one another and my aunt had the not too pleasant job of clearing out their house. In the small front room was a collection of plastic bags piled high on the floor and on the furniture. In the plastic bags were stuffed…more and more plastic bags, 100s, if not thousands of them. The couple must have kept every plastic bag they were ever given in any shop or in any supermarket they had ever been to.

The collections made by May Savidge of Wells by the Sea were even more remarkable, and in some ways, had a value beyond anything she herself would have conceived. The reason for her collecting habit is obscure but perhaps she had more reason than most of us to want to hang onto the past and she kept hold of almost everything she had ever had from her teenage years onwards, from love letters to joiners' bills, from bus tickets to bottle tops.

When she died, she left her house to her nephew and his wife, Tony and Christine Adams. They knew that she was a hoarder, but what they found when they entered her house after her death was beyond imagining. They pushed open the front door with difficulty because behind it was, 'a pale green 1930s kitchen unit. Tony opened its doors to find that it contained 100s of neatly stacked empty jam jars, large and small, ancient and modern, glass and pottery.'

This was just the beginning. They were to find room after room stacked to the ceiling with just a narrow walkway between the packing cases and cardboard boxes; but as in the kitchen cupboard, the chaos was orderly. Everything was sorted into categories and everything was labelled.

Although May had started keeping a diary from the age of 13, it was from 8th November 1946 onwards that she started on the 440 numbered volumes, set out like account books, in which she recorded her daily life in great detail. From these and the hoard of labels, packets, files, receipts, containers (100s of matchboxes were stored inside old soap cartons, Omo, Oxydol and others), newspapers, magazines and every letter she ever received, every leaflet dropped through her letterbox – from these all aspects of her life was documented. 100s of empty paracetamol blister packs were found in one box, and on each was the number of tablets she took, with the date and the hour, all stored neatly in date order. In her account book, she recorded the tins of dog food she bought and how much she paid for them. She would then remove the labels and use the back of them to write her shopping lists – she was into recycling long before it became popular.

Although like Daisy Bates, she had a conscientious dedication to making accurate records, May Savidge had no social purpose in mind, no sense of a valuable legacy in what she was doing. It was entirely personal and may perhaps be explained by searing losses earlier in her life, of her father when she was ten years old and of a man she met when she was 16 and whom she dearly loved, but who died before they were able to get married. It may be fanciful, but perhaps, just perhaps, she could not bear the loss of anything more.

It is not just for this not entirely unusual obsession with keeping records and hoarding personal possessions that May Savidge is to be remembered, but an achievement much more remarkable She, almost singlehandedly, moved a house. She dismantled it brick by brick, tile by tile, wooden beam by wooden beam, and reassembled it about 100 miles away. It received considerable publicity at the time, but the story has been told in detail by Christine Adams, who eventually finished the work that May started.

May was 59 when the move began at the end of a 15-year battle with Ware Council, who wanted to demolish her house to build a relief road. The house was not only a listed building, but many thought, as did May, that it was of exceptional historic importance. It was a small medieval hall house, a house built with a large central hall rising to the roof which had a hole in it to let out the smoke from the central fire. In Tudor times, a chimney was added, and it was then converted into two small dwellings. Her mother had bought the house for £400 some years before, and in 1954, a compulsory purchase order offered May £10 for it.

Preparing for the move, in typical fashion, every item of the structure was labelled and numbered. She had hoped to move the timber frame in one piece, but although she even contacted the Royal Airforce at Contishall, Norwich, as well as the American Air Force, they said were extremely sorry but they did not have a helicopter man enough for the job. Everything was eventually moved lorry load by lorry load onto a new site at Wells-next-the-Sea and the work of re-erection began, but not before all the nails in the beams had been removed painfully by hand. The tedious work took weeks and she set herself targets, using an alarm clock and then noted how many nails she had removed each hour.

For the next 20 years, she lived in a caravan on the site, replacing the numbered tiles and laying the numbered bricks. By 1992, the main fabric was in place and she had moved into the house, living in a small kitchen heated by an idiosyncratic Rayburn, difficult to light and difficult to keep alight. There was only a ladder to the upper rooms, which she was finding it difficult to climb and she presumably slept in a chair in the kitchen. The windows were just covered in plastic. She was often cold, tired and hungry, but she never complained. Although she lived on her own, she was always sociable, wrote many letters to friends and interested enquirers and welcomed many intrigued visitors. With bent back, frequent giddy fits, ulcerated legs and numerous other health problems, she kept going until a few months before her death. It was Christine who eventually finished off her work and wrote up her life. Ware Hall House in now a small guest house run by Christine.

Although May had been invited to a Buckingham Palace Garden party, it meant nothing to some of the people of Wells-next-the-Sea, who were anything but complimentary about her. They were heard to call her a 'fly old bird' or a 'bag lady', and the local boys taunted her and pushed bangers through her letter box. Some thought her mad or at least that she was suffering from obsessive compulsive disorder, but according to Christine, neither were true.

As she says, and no one knew her better, "I think she was odd, unusual, eccentric, yes… but that she was oddly, unusually and eccentrically virtuous."

"She wasn't frightened of death, but she found living with loss almost unbearable."

"Her thriftiness allowed her to be generous – her accounts record countless payments to any number of charities."3

It was her public spirit that led her to work early in her life for the St Johns Ambulance and local old people's welfare associations and it was her love of heritage and her hatred of bureaucracy that led her to fight to save the building she cherished above all other things in the latter years of her life. She did not live to see the work she had started completed, and her final word to Christine was, 'Sorry', knowing that in her will she had left Christine with the burden of completing the restoration of the house. That was no easy task and cost Christine her marriage, but in the end, Christine knew how much she owed to her aunt and felt she could only say to her, 'Thank you.'

Dr David Weeks[4], a neuroscientist at Edinburgh Royal Hospital, suspects that eccentrics are less prone to mental illness than everyone else. People with a mental illness 'suffer' from their behaviour, but he believes that rather than suffering, eccentrics are quite happy people.

Hooray for eccentricity!

Chapter 5 Notes

1. Chouinard, Yvon (2006) Let My People Go Surfing: The Education of a Reluctant Businessman) Penguin Books, London
2. Bates, Daisy (2011) The Passing of the Aborigines Theophana See also Blackburn, Julia. (1994) Daisy Bates in the Desert: A Woman's Life Among the Aborigines London, Secker & Warburg.
3. Adams, Christine and McMahon, Michael, 2009, A lifetime in the Building, Aurum Press Ltd, London
4. Weeks, David and James, Jamie (1995) Eccentrics: A study of Sanity and Strangeness, Phoenix 4500 words

Chapter 6
Minor Frailties

Old age has all the disadvantages, loss of hearing, loss of sight, no longer able to learn, becoming forgetful, general discontent.

A classical description of the infirmities of old age

On other hand, Clive Anderson could say, "This is the month I turn 70, and I have never felt more energetic… Perhaps it is because extra room has been created in my cerebellum by the fading sex impulse. Somebody once said that a young heterosexual male thinks about sex once every 30 seconds… I calculate that my rate is now down to about once a minute."

A friend said to me the other day, "When did you start to feel old?"

She was a good friend, so I resisted the temptation to say, "How dare you suggest I am old!"

My honest answer would have been, "When I was seventeen and got my driving licence," or, "Perhaps it was the day I knew I was pregnant."

It was certainly not the day I retired. That was the beginning of something new, something I had never experienced before – of being paid not to go to work.

That is the view of many who live in western society, in the early 21st century, those who not only expect a pension but know the date when it will be theirs by right, however big or small, until the day they die. This is completely contrary to what happens in most of the rest of the world and what happened in the past. It may not even be true for the future. Perhaps we will need to return to the idea that retirement is not a cut-off point but that growing old is a continuous process.

So, for most people in the world, becoming old is not a date or an event, but a gradual process, often unmarked in any significant way. The non-life-threatening infirmities of old age creep up on you and most people as they grow older have some trouble with getting upstairs, with remembering names, with forgetting birthdays, with hearing or with sight, and even with the sense of touch, smell and taste. Somehow, the fingers are no longer quite as sensitive as once they were and fiddling for change in one's purse is a minor frustration, but an embarrassing one as the queue of youngsters behind you hide their sniggers. But young people may be surprised to learn that learning to cope is often not so much a cause for anxiety or rage (as it very often is if such disabilities occur at a young age), but a challenge to one's own ability to solve problems. Apprehension gives way to acceptance. A parallel may be found in a teenager who discovers his or her body has unexpected bulges or unexpected hair growth, and who at first is severely embarrassed by it, but who soon learns to live with it. The apprehension goes, and for most people, the loss of childhood is balanced by the excitement of growing up and the acceptance of the inevitability of change. For older people, the changes are accompanied not so much by excitement as by a certain detachment, a tranquillity that is difficult to explain, but that perhaps derives from the experiences that you have so far managed to survive; so you even exalt in leaving behind the anxieties of youth and middle age.

As Jonathan Swift said, "No wise man ever wished to be younger."

That is not to say that as people get older, they no longer grumble, a word that rhymes with mumble, implying a lowkey backdrop to life's important conversations. Grumbling is a treasured perquisite of being old – grumbling about the minor irritations of life – such as opening bottles and packets and coping with electronic gadgets, as well as more important things such as the selfishness of children, the rudeness of shop assistants or the threatening behaviour of teenagers. 'It wasn't like this in my day!' So when did the older generation ever fail to criticise the ways of the young?

That the challenges of coping with the minor infirmities of old age may sometimes be daunting goes without saying. If you are unlucky enough to have lost all your teeth, initially there is a deep, deep feeling of loss. Something has gone which was a vital part of you and it will never come back. Looking in the mirror, you are horrified to see the hollow where your teeth once were. But gradually, if you have a good set of dentures, you begin to crow, "No more visits to the dentist!", "No more poking into my mouth to see if I have a black hole in my tooth."

You do not anymore feel mental anguish when you realise you forgot to brush your teeth after breakfast. After dinner will do just as well. Some philosophers such as Philipe de Navarre saw additional 'advantages.'

"The very ageing of the body prevents the person from committing the most heinous of crimes. Having lost his teeth, the old man will laugh less, gnaw less at the good name of others and talk less." [1]

There are always downsides of course; like the day I threw my dentures on the fire with some orange peel, without realising it. It doesn't pay to take out your teeth and put them on the stool beside you while enjoying a little telly in the evening. I did not discover it until next day, when they were unusable. It so happened I was due to face a room full of people that evening to whom I was giving a talk. I remembered too late the advice given to lecturers, 'Always keep a second set of dentures!'

It is said that there are very few characteristics that distinguish man from other mammals, but one of them is that most other mammals (not all) do not laugh. We do not know whether or not they have a sense of humour, but it is not expressed by laughter. There is another distinguishing trait, although I know of no investigation into it, and that is that many other mammals appear to have something humans have not: an interest in, and a passion for, the scent other animals' urine. A dog knows no greater joy – at least that is the impression given by my dog – of scenting out the marks left by other dogs, and then overprinting them with their own signature.

For humans, it is the reverse and the scent of urine, especially the pee of old people is repulsive. We may happily ignore the wrinkles, the crooked back, the flat feet of an old person we know, but smell is a much more difficult barrier to overcome. How much more then is an old person aware of the difficulties of bladder control that seem to increase with age. Sometimes, of course, it is a medical problem that can be overcome by surgery. Sometimes it just seems to be a failure of communication between the person and their bladder, or rather that the bladder starts to dominate the dialogue. Tony Benn, aged 82, gives a wonderful description of this in his published diary.

Sunday 24 March 2007

As soon as I got off the bus at Notting Hill Gate, my bladder knew it was approaching home, and although it behaved quite well on the tube, the nearer it got to home, the more it began to cause me anxiety. When I put the key in the door, the bladder got the message that it's almost over and so as I opened the door I rushed to the back corridor. I kept talking to my bladder seriously saying, "We're nowhere near the lavatory," but it knew more than I did. I got there and just managed to relieve myself. But funny, I think it has a satellite navigation system.[2]

It may be helpful to know that for some people there is such a thing as control of mind over matter. For others, it simply means developing the habit of noting where the next toilet will be or knowing how much coffee to drink before going on a bus. Like young children, when you go to someone's house for the first time, you are always inquisitive to know where the bathroom is and cannot wait to inspect it.

Having to wear a hearing aid or to wear glasses for the first time or having to walk with a stick, you feel as though you are announcing to the world that you are getting old, a signal you would prefer not to be giving out, whatever you are feeling. Then you discover that George W Bush, when he was president of the USA, always wore hearing aids; and that it is now the fashion for young walkers to show off with their Scandinavian walking poles. So, now, when you notice that many of the youngsters are walking up and down the street, wearing hearing aids attached to their e-players and swinging their walking poles, suddenly you feel far less conspicuous.

It is still possible to live a rewarding life, even if there is a complete hearing loss, or if the loss of sight is severe, as we know from those who have experienced it most of their lives.

Helen Keller who lived to be 88 years old, once said, "The most beautiful things in the world cannot be seen, or even touched, but just felt in the heart."[3]

Helen Keller knew what she was talking about. She was not only blind but deaf from the age of two. She was born in 1880 in a small town in Alabama, a perfectly normal baby in every way. Her parents could not have envisaged that at two years old, an illness, possibly meningitis, would leave her both deaf and blind and turn her into a little monster. She was completely out of control, smashing china and kicking and screaming on the floor in rages that terrified the whole household. She must have felt the fierce anger that any of us might feel when being struck by an unfair and inexplicable infirmity, but she had no means of expressing it, except through rage. It seemed her family would never be able to cope and they considered putting her into an institution.

Helen had a remarkable intelligence and she amazed everyone. She learned to type on both an ordinary and a braille typewriter. Accompanied by her tutor and friend, Anne, she was able to go to college, Radcliffe College, where she was the first deaf-blind person to gain a Bachelor of Arts degree. Her passion for life led her to take up many causes, including the suffragette movement and the campaign for birth control. She tirelessly campaigned for the blind, many of whom were placed in asylums, a fate she narrowly escaped herself. She travelled throughout the States, giving lectures.

During her long life, she was able, among other things, to lecture worldwide, to write bestseller books and to found an international research organisation. She was eventually awarded by President Lyndon Johnson the Presidential Medal of Freedom, the highest civilian award in America.

But it seems that highly intelligent though she was, there were other factors at work. Perhaps because she was blind her brain was not cluttered up with sights and sounds that fill our days, so her ability to concentrate on what she was able to do was magnified. She had an intense love of life, that part of life that was available to her.

"Life is a daring adventure or nothing," she was able to say, "If I, deaf and blind, find life rich and interesting, how much more can you gain by the use of your five senses."

Her disability made her determined, a trait that is seen again and again in the disabled. She once said, "We can do anything we want if we stick at it long enough."

Her life offers many lessons, even for those who do not experience disability until later in life. No one knew better than Helen that we are living in a world which requires two-way communication. We can understand how important that must have been for her.

She said, "We are never really happy, until we brighten the lives of others."

She recognised that man is a social animal and she refused to allow her disabilities to isolate her, "Alone we can do so little, together we can do so much."

Her early years had made her acutely aware of the horrors of isolation.

For many people, to be part of the wider community is an imperative and a joy. I am reminded of an elderly person I knew who walked badly and had little hearing, but her eyes were good. Every time she took her dog for a walk, she took two plastic bags, one for the dog mess, of course, but in the other she put all the litter she came across. She was doing her bit for the community she lived in. I think Helen was saying that everyone can do something, whatever their disabilities, even if it is just a smile from a sickbed.

Another friend of mine, we will call her Jane, had given up the idea of marriage to look after her father and then her mother, who were both ill during the middle years of Jane's life. Not only had her love life to be abandoned but she had limited opportunity for a social life. Yet, despite her circumstances, she was never without friends. She attended every village function whenever she could and never missed watching the annual village sports. She knew everyone, their family history and the names of all their children. When she was nearly 90, she suddenly went almost blind, but somehow managed to walk Main Street with her white stick, feeling for the edge of the pavement. When people stopped to talk, as they always did, she peered into their faces until she recognised them. She often had to ask you to speak a little louder as she was anxious not to miss the latest gossip. Once or twice, she had a fall and broke her arm, but weeks later she was back in circulation, ever wanting to hear the latest news about your family. She could no longer make the little pots of lemon curd she used to give away as presents, but what she did have to give you was far more valuable, than just a jar of lemon curd. She may have only become deaf and blind towards the end of her life, but in spirit she was another Helen Keller.

People who knew Jane brightened when they saw her walking towards them, but I wonder what a stranger who happened to pass by her would think – if they even noticed her. She would be placed in the stereotypical category of old and useless. Anne Widdecombe, who was looking after her elderly mother remonstrated with her usual vigour when someone suggested she was her mother's carer.

"I am NOT her carer," she said, "I am her daughter!"

Labels say so much and so little. They say something about the person that uses the label; they speak little of reality.

It was ever thus. From classical time onwards, there are some very cruel descriptions of the old, written by the young. 'Men old as you are such lovers of life, who ought to be eager for death as a remedy for the evils of old age.'[4]

It expresses the puzzlement of the young that, judging from appearances, it seems impossible that old age can be enjoyed. It also perhaps hints at the fear of old age, as if the very presence of someone who looks old has no right to stay around to remind younger people of what is to come.

Together with fat people and mothers-in-law, old people are often the butt of jokes, although perhaps less so now than in the days of the music hall and the naughty seaside postcard. An old man just arriving downstairs for breakfast, says to his wife, "You look wonderful this morning, darling. Have you seen my glasses?"

A lady says to her elderly husband, "Let's go upstairs for a little…excitement…"

The husband replies, "Which is it to be? I can't do both."

These jokes poke fun at infirmity and often hint at the lechery of old men, but surprisingly, I find that old people are quite ready to laugh at them, and the men laugh the loudest. Most of the time, old people (but not those who are approaching old age, and who are not ready to admit it) are prepared to laugh at themselves, and they no longer get angry because of what people think. Some may even take advantage of it! A mother-in-law, perfectly capable of getting up from her chair, says to her daughter-in-law, "Could you turn the telly on for me? There's a dear."

They give up trying to change other people's misconceptions and decide they might as well make use of it. After all, the young have no experience of being old!

But even old people among themselves may be guilty of misunderstanding others whom they do not know intimately. At a meeting recently, I sat alongside a lady whose invisible presence had failed to register with me on previous occasions. In nondescript clothes – was it a grey tweed suit or was it a washed-out blue? I am sure she wasn't wearing trousers – or was she? She was completely unremarkable and unmemorable. I had greeted her on a previous occasion, but as she was so obviously deaf, I made no attempt to engage her further.

This time, I passed her a pamphlet that had been passed to me. She passed it back to me, saying, "I can't read it."

She said it in a matter-of-fact voice and seemed not at all irritated. She did not even ask what it was about. My first thought was, *What a waste of time. What does she come for anyway?*

Then my second thought was that perhaps it was really quite sensible, and perhaps how lucky she was. We are bombarded all the time with information we really do not need and perhaps do not even want to know. I was not really better informed after I had read that piece of paper and I would promptly forget it.

Her response made me curious, so I thought that if I moved closer and spoke clearly, I might be able to learn more. "How do you manage?" I asked, rather condescendingly.

"Oh, I'm fine, I've got my daughter."

"Do you live with her?"

"Oh no, she lives at Burton (some six miles away). I go to lunch there every Sunday."

"So, you live on your own?"

"Oh yes. I use a lot of ready meals and cook them in the microwave."

"What do you do with yourself all day?"

"I do watch telly. If I get close to the screen, I can see well enough."

"I guess you watch soaps?"

"No, I can't be bothered with them. I like Eggheads and Mastermind. I quite often know the answers. And I like documentaries."

I eventually discovered she had been a maths teacher and had travelled widely. When I asked her age, she said, "I'll have to think."

It took her a while, but clearly her maths had not deserted her. She could remember which year she was born and what the present year was and was working it out, "Yes, I'm 87 now. I don't bother to keep count."

In our early years, age is very important to us. It marks our progression towards the adult world. Being ten years old is very different from being nine. Then 18 is an important landmark. After that, 21. Beyond that, it is every ten years that requires celebration or commiseration, with banner headlines on a local roundabout. 'Jack is 40!' But old people have at last got age into perspective.

Because she did not walk very well, my new chum was brought to the meeting by a friend. I was still wondering why she came, but I did not like to ask her. When she got up to go, she thanked me very warmly and I then knew the answer. She may not want bits of paper to read, giving her bits of information that were useless to her, telling her about outings she could not go on and talks she could not hear, but this meeting was a pleasant afternoon out with pleasant people she had got to know, and poor eyesight or not, she was happy to knit a few squares for a blanket for the poor children in Africa. Comradeship; being useful; that was still what life was all about. For me, she was no longer an invisible person in the front row, she was an ordinary, possibly an extraordinary person, with a personality and a history.

When you are really not bothered about how old you are, then you have conquered ageing. You as old as you feel, not as old as other people think you are. That latter is a dangerous road to take.

Throughout our lives, others have shaped the way we think about ourselves and even in old age, we cannot escape from this. Over 30 years ago, in 1979, a professor of psychology in America, Ellen Langer[5], was interested to test out how our thoughts may be influenced by those around us and how those thoughts might affect our bodies. She selected a number of men all over 75 and from various backgrounds, who, while not ill, were quite frail, and were being cared for. They were taken by bus, with suitcases packed for a week's stay, to a house where they were told they would live as they would have done 20 years before. Apart from the 50s decor, they had wireless (radio) and TV programmes from the 50s, discussed 50s events as if they were current, watched 50s films and listened to 50s music. They were left to look after themselves and encouraged to behave as they would have behaved when they were 20 years younger. If they could not carry their suitcase up to the bedroom, they had to solve the problem themselves, usually by taking out the contents and carrying them up in small loads.

Before the week's experiment, they were all tested for sight, hearing, dexterity and so on. At the end of the week when they were retested, Professor Langer was amazed at the extent and type of change. Their average blood pressure had dropped, their IQ test showed a higher score, their movement and gait had improved, even their sight and hearing had improved. This experiment was repeated recently in the UK, using well known, but elderly personalities and their experience was televised. The results were exactly the same.

Professor Langer concluded that if people are treated as capable, autonomous individuals, that is the way they will act. If they think of themselves as being in control, they will take over control. On the other hand, if they are treated as incompetent, they will, either out of wilfulness or frustration, accept dependence. Professor Langer undertook further experiments in old people's homes that confirmed the findings that changing the age you think you are affects your symptoms of ageing. She even hypothesised that most people will live as long as they think they will live, a hypothesis not yet proven!

So, as old age approaches, you could say that there are two main schools of thought:

1. 'I Intend to live to be a burden'
2. 'Getting old is not scary. I will have none of this'

Anonymous quotes

When it comes to dealing with minor disabilities, there never has been a time when there have been so many devices, appliances, opportunities, practical help and concessions to assist in overcoming the inconveniences that come with the ageing body. Be it an optometrist or an optician, a dentist or an orthodontist, an osteopath or a chiropractor, a homoeopath or an aromatherapist, there is a great deal of help available that was unheard of 50 years ago. You suffer incontinence occasionally; there is help to be had. The number and variety of stair lifts and motorised wheelchairs is amazing and cater for all kinds of situations. A 70-year-old couple I know now have bicycles powered by batteries, replacing their pedal-powered cycles.

There are also plenty of exercise opportunities even if you do not expect. You can run a marathon at the age of 100; from swimming to walking the dog; from gentle dancing to Tai Chi. There are activities to suit all tastes and levels of ability. Gardening is a great activity. A friend of mine has had a hip and a knee operation, so she now does her gardening sitting on a low brick wall. She assures me it is most therapeutic. If you feel the cold more than in the past, no one need know how many layers you hide under you very fashionable flowing dress. It is not only old people who are recommended to take an afternoon nap. My own mother always went to bed for half an hour after lunch from about the age of 30 onwards. No one complained.

You begin not to care about what people think and the solutions for many disabilities are there if you look for them and have the courage. All you need is the knowledge, a positive attitude and sometimes the ability to pay for them.

As Helen Keller said, "The marvellous richness of human experience would lose something of rewarding joy if there were no limitations to overcome."

But both Jane and Helen Keller came from the affluent west and they were speaking to relatively affluent people. It is salutary to remember that such choices, even here in the west, are not open to everyone and in most of the world, such thoughts are not only flippant but insulting. Such a view of old age is not only undreamed of but unheard of. Although in some parts of the world, the care of the elderly by their families compensates to some extent for the lack of opportunities available in western society, for many, the prospect of old age must be quite terrifying. To grow old is inevitable. To grow old and to be poor is perhaps the greatest of all tragedies. For so many living in the third world in direst poverty, just staying alive means labouring or begging until there is no life left, just a body stretched out on the street.

Yet, when I was travelling amongst the very poor in the so-called third world, I was taken completely by surprise at the attitude of the people we met in the slum areas. They were not only cheerful, with a ready smile and always a joke, but appeared to bear no grudge, to harbour no anger. That is a generalisation, of course, and there would be those overwhelmed by depression or anxiety, but most had learned to accept that which they could not change.

The same seems to be true of old people everywhere. Many have instinctively learned to accommodate, without rancour and with humour, to the frailties encountered in growing old. Very many enjoy their old age. This conclusion is supported by the longitudinal study of ageing by Baltimore University. Personality, it seems, does not change with age.

'With aging, a human personality remains remarkable stable. An individual who is cheerful and optimistic when young usually remains so throughout life. On the other hand, someone who is unusually grouchy and mean in early life keeps the same personality traits in later life.'[6]

The young hypochondriac will become the elderly woman who takes up part-time residence in the doctor's surgery; a young person with a matter-of-fact attitude to health will suffer the minor infirmities of old age with dignity, and yes, even a touch of humour.

Chapter 6 Notes

1. Thane, Pat (ed), 2005 The Long History of Old Age p 94 (quoting Philipe de Navarre, les quartres ages de l' hommes) Thames and Hudson, London
2. Benn Tony, 2007, More Time for Politics, Hutchinson, London
3. Helen Keller quotations from quotationspage.com et al
4. Lucien, Dialogues of the Dead, quoted p 57 The Long History of Old Age, Pat Thane (ed), 2005, Thames and Hudson Ltd London
5. Langer, Ellen, J, 2009, Counterclockwise, Ballantyne Books, New York
6. Nathan W. Shock, T.Frankland Williams and James I. Fozard, Older and Wiser, 1989, Baltimore Longitudinal Study of Aging, NIH, Washington D.C. Government Printing Office

Chapter 7
Mutton Dressed as Lamb

Isn't she wonderful for her age! Ugh! What has old age got to do with it?

Helen Mirren

In the Middle Ages, authors and preachers made, 'critical and sarcastic comments on the vain efforts of old women to conceal their decline with lavish clothing, cosmetics and feminine wiles.'

Shulamith Shaha

If I had had changes done to my face, I would not have had the part of the Queen Mother (in Stephen Frears, 'The Queen'). You never know when your best part is coming.

Sylvia Simms

As we saw in the last chapter, Ellen Langer[1], the psychology professor at Harvard University, suggests we are surrounded by subtle suggestions that old age is both inevitable and a period of irreversible decline. These signals encourage us to dress as old people. This, in turn, reinforces the feeling that perhaps we are indeed old and decrepit. She also checked out older people whose lives demanded a uniform – nurses and soldiers. She found that people who wore a uniform to work and who were of the same economic status as a control group, had fewer days off work, fewer visits to the doctor and fewer chronic diseases. She concluded that this was because they were not constantly reminded of their age by their clothes.

There may be some truth in this, but surely it is an oversimplification and it might be that it was not so much their uniform, but the demands of their job, the rewards it offered them and their continued confidence in doing it well because of the experience they brought to it that accounted for the difference.

So how do people dress when they are old, and why? Assuming we have the money, do we have a free choice, and if so, how do we choose? Or are we constrained by invisible forces outside our conscious control?

In the 21st century, fashion becomes ever more dominant in our lives, whether it is the colour of our bathroom suite, the style of our mobile phones, the cushions that decorate our beds, or the design of babies' pushchairs. Clothes change season by season and are determined by the social group you belong to, the area you live in, the university you go to or of course, your age. Fashion is, by definition, something that changes, but never before has it changed so frequently. In the past and even in a few parts of the world even yet that have not caught up with the west (what a loaded phrase that is), fashion was and still is slow to change. Clothing and body decoration have always been used to indicate age or status, or to announce your membership of a particular group or tribe. The tattooing of a Maori man in front of his ears showed he was married, while it was fashionable for a Xhosa woman from South Africa to carry a beaded bag around her waist that held all her accessories for smoking. This indicated she was married, as only married women were allowed to smoke. Presumably, learning to smoke was part of the excitement of the marriage ceremonial. There would be an individual component to the design of the bag, but it would follow certain well-known rules of design and like the Maori tattoo, fashion would change over time. Contact with westerners brought new kinds of beads, which would lead to fashion changes, led by those who could afford to buy the beads, but changes were seldom so frequent, so startling or so imperative as they are for the young of today in western society.

In China in the early days of Communism, departure in even in a small detail from the uniform prescribed by the state – that is the Mao-collared jacket with green or blue baggy trousers, for men and women – marked you out as someone who secretly harboured capitalist ideas. Fashion was a symbol of western decadence. With everyone wearing the same clothes, there was no distinction of class, group affiliation or of your age. This was in startling contrast to what had gone before in China and was an obvious reaction against it. The official dress at the Chinese court was not only flamboyant, but it had to be appropriate to the status of the individual, the type of occasion, the season and even the time of the month. In China today, attitude to dress and fashion has changed yet again. The elderly still cling to modified versions of the Mao uniform, but the younger generation like to be 'cool', which means aping whatever from the west appeals to them. This sometimes gets out of hand. A teacher of English in a Chinese university had to be gently reprimanded by her principal for wearing a long topless evening dress while giving her lectures. She obviously wanted to appear 'cool' to her young students.

We all, even in China, now have a freedom unknown to previous generations. 'Choice' is the buzzword, but is our choice as Ellen Langer claims far more constrained than we imagine? Do we really at some point as we get older, sit down and think, *Yes, now I am 50, 60 or 70: this is the way I should dress*?

I think it is more likely that as with the older communists, many of us continue to dress perhaps not as we did in our youth but certainly as we dressed in our middle years. I can remember when the New Look came in after the Second World War. Clothes rationing applied not only to dresses and coats but to fabric to make up clothes. At one time, even pleats were outlawed.

Many a wedding dress was made out of parachute silk which could be 'obtained' without using clothing coupons. The New Look, introduced by Christian Dior in the late forties, just as clothes rationing was abolished, was a reaction against the austerity of wartime. He sometimes used up to 20 yards of material in his creations, which had mid-calf hemlines, and wide flared skirts. This was the 'look' coveted by my contemporaries. The older generation, the middle-aged, continued to wear dresses which were often shorter than knee length. Backcombing then came into fashion for teenagers but when these teenagers became middle-aged, they often continued to keep to this style of hairdressing (which made combing the hair normally quite impossible) long after the young had adopted much softer styles. Today, it is the elderly who go in for permed hair so popular in their youth. I had my first perm at seventeen, quite a horrific experience, being wired up to a machine with an extra-terrestrial feel about it. At that time, unless you had naturally curly hair, a perm was a necessity.

Even if people do not sit down and consciously decide what it is now appropriate for them to wear at their age in order to produce the image they want to offer the public, those decisions do have to be made every time we go clothes shopping, whether it is on the high street or at a West End couturier. The decisions are important, but I believe with Ellen Langer, they are not entirely under our conscious control. There are too many accidents of birth, the fortuity of birth right, circumstances of upbringing and experiences of life for the decision to be an uninfluenced choice. Who knows why one person will say, 'I like this', while another will say, 'I like that.'

I often wonder about those persuaded by Gok Won[2], the TV fashion guru, who transforms the image of very ordinary ladies who crave a makeover, if they continue to dress in the style he proposes for them. For the audience, the person appears to undergo a radical change, but does that really happen? For those already interested in style, perhaps all they needed was some tuition on how to adapt this year's fashion to their own figure. That's fine. But if they happened to be the kind of person who was persuaded to take part in the experiment by family and friends, but who had never in the past enjoyed dressing in a way that made them stand out in a crowd, I would not be surprised if they clung to their old wardrobe.

While I identified eagerly with these caterpillars turned into butterflies in Gok Wan's programmes, I must admit that I shrink from dressing in a way that turns people's heads. But then I think I could never be persuaded to go on the programme. For I am one of those for whom choosing clothes has always been a problem – no worse, an agony – and I have been surprised to find that I am not the only one. I think it started as a teenager when acne produced horrid pustules on my face and left scars. I had a distrust of makeup, having seen those who had tried to disguise their disfigurement. For me, their attempts appeared worse than failure, for it seemed to produce a visage from a horror movie.

Added to that was the certain knowledge that from the sideways view in the mirror, I had a rear that looked like East Anglia on a map of Britain (I was keen on geography at the time). When I now look at a photograph of myself aged seventeen, I hardly recognise it; this girl really looks quite pretty, if not exactly beautiful. I was also frightened of men, having had an unpleasant experience with what these days would be called a paedophile (I have been surprised at how many of many contemporaries are at last admitting for the first time to a similar experience). To preen my feathers or ogle the boys seemed to me a very dangerous activity. So, my inclination has always been to dress well enough to avoid critical comment, but not so well that it also called for superlative comment. I do admit though to a rosy feeling if someone should say, 'I like your dress.'

Discussing this with a group of women, not all old women, I discovered that quite a few of them had the same attitude to clothes as I did myself, although their reasons for a lack of interest in fashion may have been different. Does this sound quite a revolutionary concept in this century when fashion rules? Almost a criminal confession? Having admitted they did not particularly enjoy shopping for clothes, they did say that buying something for a special occasion, such as for a wedding could be exciting but did not always turn out successfully. One confessed to an addiction to buying shoes, though not on the Imelda Marcos scale. Most agreed they tried to dress in a way that was appropriate for the occasion. One remarked that she no longer wore a hat to church as she would have done years ago, but she did put on lipstick because going to church was still a special occasion. I think we are the silent majority and I think I can spot among a crowd of youngsters those who dress to be part of the crowd and those who always aim to be at the forefront of fashion.

Perhaps we are the 'real old people' that Tim Lott [3] referred to in an article in the Observer. These are 'the old dears', 'with fusty hats, pastel rinsed hair, heavy overcoats worn in summer and sensible if not surgical shoes', 'with their endless cups of tea and ginger nuts'; although some of my crowd prefer coffee and shortbreads. A group of schoolchildren, asked by Jane Miller[4] to describe their grandparents came up with a similar picture, using the adjectives, 'small, 'bent', 'shuffling', but one also added 'kindly.' Tim Lott actually mourns their loss and declares they have now been replaced by a generation of old men in bright Bermuda shorts and old women in designer clothes, with the blue rinse replaced by blond streaks. They are he suggests leftovers from the Swinging Sixties, who have not quite come to terms with how they should behave. While Tim claims to want to become a 'real old person' himself, he is hardly encouraging or prejudice free. Will he really want to be called an 'old dear' or an 'old geezer'? I think not.

I do not want to give the impression that everyone in my group was uninterested in fashion. Among them there were several for whom fashion always had been and still was important. Their wardrobes consumed a significant portion of their income. Their clothes were stylish, and what was particularly true of the older people, they were stylish in the way they wore them. It distinguished them out as people for whom appearance had always been a matter of pride.

A 24-year-old designer, Fanny Karst 5, born in France, but who studied and worked in England, became aware of the demand for fashion by older people. Her models are aged between 60 and 80, and it is to her credit that one observer[6] commenting on the decidedly fashionable styles she had designed for these white-haired old ladies said, "The clothes are so good that you are drawn not to the fabric but to the women."

They not only appear elegant and attractive, but their age gives them a timeless quality, missing on younger, flashier models. The fabrics are often cross cut or draped from the shoulder, with a pattern down the centre, drawing the eye away from the edges. The shoes are so stylish that you are not aware that the heels are not high. The whole image is one of deception, of trompe d'oeil.

One collection is labelled 'Ladies Rebellion', and the signature garment is a silver bomber jacket worn over a white t-shirt that proclaims in large capital letters, 'NOT AT YOUR AGE.' Some challenge! I showed a picture of the model to some teenagers and asked them to tell me the first thought that came into their minds. While the words, 'unexpected' and 'out of the ordinary' were predictable, one responded without hesitation and with some vehemence, 'shocking!' Of course the image was meant to shock, but the immediacy and the vigour of the response had more in it of disapproval than of surprise, something I had not expected from this quite sensible teenager. It is perhaps impossible to eradicate from the young their perception of how they expect the old to behave. Perhaps we should give up trying. Even the reaction of the middle-aged mother of the teenager was, 'just silly, inappropriate.'

It was noted that one year at the Latitude Pop Festival, there was a woman suitably dressed for the occasion, with green wellies and rock band t-shirt. Her shorts were the regulation denim cut-offs which revealed, as they would, her thighs. The woman was about 50 years old, so her blotched skin and all too visible veins did credit to a working life, but not to her image. The comments of passersby were not complimentary.

It has ever been thus. In the 17th century, Lady Sarah Cowper 7, a person of rank, was highly critical of the attempts of some of her contemporaries to improve their image. In her diary, she wrote upon the way a friend of hers comported herself, *I met with Lady W..., of whom it may be said hath rent her face with painting. She is at least as old as I am* (she was in her 50s) *and hugely infirm yet affects the follies and aires of youth, displays her breasts and ears, adorns both with sparkling gems while her eies look dead, skin shrivell'd, cheeks sunk, shaking head, trembling hands, and all things bidd shut up shop and leave to traffick with such vanities or affectation of superfluities which signify nothing but weakness.*

There are those of course who age gracefully and manage to deceive us into thinking that they are much younger than their age. Such is Sheer Sandon who starred in *The Rock Horse Picture Show* in 1975 and who in 1995 won an Oscar for her performance as a nun in *Dead Man Walking*.

During her life, she revelled in sex and drugs as do most Hollywood stars and was a fan of Rock 'n' Roll, so she hardly led the life of a nun. Now at 63, after having had three kids, the first when she was 39, she looks little over 40. The smooth skin of her shoulders and face give away little of her age. Cast as a grandmother in her latest film, *The Lovely Bones*, I guess she will be a challenge to the make-up artist.

For many women, especially those in modelling and acting, to retain young looks becomes an obsession, an obsession propelled by the need to find work. As someone in the marketing industry once said, "Old faces don't sell."

Come the demand, come the solution; and the demand comes not only from actresses. Tinkering with bums, boobs and Botox is a burgeoning industry. A single company, Transform, which offers a whole range of procedures, from volumisation ('mature patients are like balloons that need blowing up') to breast implants, hormone replacement therapy and anti-ageing cosmetics, currently has a £40 million a year turnover. And for men, there are hair transplants where up to 2000 hairs are placed in individual hair follicles by a team of three working in 20-minute shifts. The marketing is intensive with phone call operators offering free trials that lead to treatments that run into many thousands of pounds.

The hard sell is aimed at vulnerable people, who often have low self-esteem. It is not so much, 'We can make you look beautiful,' but, 'This is for you and no one else,' or,

'What's important is how you feel about yourself'. This is the 'because you deserve it' culture. Transform has been going for 35 years and looks to grow even bigger.

It is just as well you feel good about yourself at the end of your costly treatment, for when your friends look at you, they may have some reservations. Suzanne Somers, actor turned cosmetics businesswoman, has undergone many treatments herself over the years, and some would say she is an amazing advertisement for the solutions she offers. Others are less complimentary. A little boy who happened to see her in the street, tugged at his mother's sleeve, and said, "Mum! That woman looks weird."

It is the kind of comment I have heard from other children peering at a botoxed face. One might say not so much mutton dressed up as lamb as ham pumped up with water.

But are those of us who would never contemplate transformation by drugs or cosmetic surgery right to be critical? It is likely that our view of ourselves is largely a reflection of the views others have of us. Edna O'Brien[8], the novelist, has a remarkable presence, even at nearly 80, and according to Rachel Cooke, at Edna's book launch she was, "Queenly and beautiful, brought to mind nothing so much as a glorious boat, coming slowly into port; the elegant prow of her nose, the blown sails of her hair, the leaden anchor of her evening bag, hanging over a crooked arm."

Yet she said at an interview with Rachel that she could never think of herself as good looking because her mother used to tell her that she was the ugliest child ever born. It had a lifelong effect. But perhaps a sibling that is constantly praised for her prettiness can suffer even greater damage. Contrary to what the Cinderella story has ingrained in our consciousness, living up to the image of being attractive, beautiful and desirable (especially if that leads to a life climbing up the Beauty Queen ladder) must create a tremendous strain, which must increase as the years go by. A highly revealing TV series, *Beauty and the Beast*, paired off models so obsessed with their appearance, that they went through a three-hour daily beauty routine, including daily injections to inflate their facial tissues, with people who had seriously discomforting facial disfigurements. No doubt the participants were carefully selected to achieve the result desired by the director, but the comparison between the lack of self-confidence in the models amounting almost to a psychotic condition and the self-assurance shown by those who had suffered a disfigurement horrid enough to cause people who passed them on the street to stare or snigger, was real enough and quite remarkable.

Being beautiful can create many problems. Marilyn Monroe, who was considered one of the most beautiful, curvaceous and glittering stars that populated Hollywood in the 1950s spent much of her life with her psychoanalyst. She neatly summed up her problem, "Men don't see me. They just set their eyes on me."

The 'not so beautiful' never have that problem. The face never gets in the way of the personality and that is some comfort to us elderly. Marilyn never lived long enough to show how she might have coped with an ageing face and an ageing figure dying, as she did, at the age of 36, from an overdose of barbiturates. Officially, it was suicide but accident or even homicide has never been ruled out. I think Lisa Jardine[9] was right when she said in a Radio 4 Woman's Hour programme, that 'older women who define themselves by their looks have more problems in coming to terms with old age.'

Perhaps the saddest part of the concentration in the 21st century on the appearance, of both men and women, is that it has led to younger and younger people seeking drastic beauty treatments and surgery. The airbrushed photos on the covers of almost every popular magazine set unobtainable standards of body shape, facial symmetry and skin burnish. Long shiny hair is seductive, so hairpieces are attached. Open appealing eyes are enticing, so the prints are touched up. Large busts sell, so busts are photographically enlarged. The photos are a mirage, but the advertisements for beauty treatments are so reassuring that young and old are sometimes convinced that maybe, just maybe, such beauty could be within their reach. Even a highly intelligent journalist such as Eva Wiseman[10], now 30 years old, is prepared to wonder out aloud, "If I was to have plastic surgery, what would I get?"

It makes you curious sometimes when you see a well-dressed stranger coming down the street, looking beautifully unreal; you wonder if she is a 50-year-old trying to look 35, or if she is a 35-year-old trying to look 40.

To say this is sad reflects my prejudices and that of many others. It assumes that my mother's constant dictum, "You must take pride in your appearance. You must make the best of yourself," had no truth in it.

And I am reminded of a lady who was dying of motor neurone disease. She was in great pain, lived in a wheelchair and knew she had not long to live. But for her, presenting an attractive – no, glamorous – appearance was supremely important. Often dressed in red, with fashionable jewellery, she was by any standards, smartly dressed. She wore designer sandals, and her toenails and fingernails were immaculately painted. We are social animals and the instinct to present the world with what we feel about ourselves is overpowering, even in such circumstances, perhaps especially in such circumstances.

When we reach the age of 50, some of us for whom clothes never were a priority in our lives, are content to wear whatever was comfortable for us in our 30s and 40s, while others want to deceive people in the high street into believing they still are in their 30s and 40s. But there is yet another group, identified by Catherine Mayer[11] as the 'amortals', a word that has quickly become currency. These are people for whom age has no meaning. They live in the present absorbed by whatever activity appeals to them at the time. They completely ignore the advice of such as the eminent French psychologist, Marie de Hennezell[12], who says, "We may be tempted to behave as if we aren't growing older…We might continue to dress like younger people, make light of our problems with memory, sight and hearing. But this does not help us to grow old in a positive way."

Amortals have the spirit of Peter Pan in them. Age is not a consideration.

Catherine Mayer suggests that amortals detach themselves from societal expectations of chronological age, "They tend to live the same way throughout their lives, however that life is lived and for as long as possible"

Defined thus, amortality may be a new word but it describes an attitude to life that is centuries old. The form it takes in any generation or any society is determined by the current culture. Catherine sees it as the legacy of the 'baby boomers', the cult of celebrity, the result of the improved health of ageing people and the opportunities for adventurous leisure activities. The cover of her book shows the silhouette of a bungee jumper. Her examples include her own father, who still does deep sea diving at 70 and of Richard Branson, who, 'never considered himself too young for any challenge... And he now shows no signs of considering himself too old for any challenge.' He completed the London marathon just before his sixtieth birthday.

But while the activities of the amortals in the late 20th and early 21st century may be new, there were many in the past who lived with the same attitudes and values. The term 'amortal' certainly did not appear in Samuel Johnson's dictionary in 1755, but he surely deserves to be known as an amortal. Johnson was a man of great learning, and in the mid-19th century was the centre of literary life in London. He was a close friend of Joshua Reynolds and worked in the king's library. King George III held him in such high esteem, the king visited the royal library to discuss literature with Johnson. It was thanks to Boswell 13, who was his friend for the last 20 years of his life that we know so much about him through his outstanding biography. According to Boswell, who met Johnson for the first time when he was 53, he had no interest whatsoever in the way he dressed or looked after himself. Encountering the great man for the first time, Boswell was shocked.

Describing the meeting, he writes that, 'It must be confessed that his apartment, and furniture and morning dress were sufficiently uncouth. His brown suit of clothes looked very rusty: he had on a little old shrivelled unpowdered wig, which was too small for his head; his shirt neck and the knees of his breeches were loose; his black worsted stockings ill drawn up; and he had a pair of unbuckled shoes by way of slippers.'14.

Samuel Johnson suffered continually from ill health. The day he was delivered, the midwife thought he was stillborn, but it seems he was, 'shaken, slapped, cajoled, yelled at and paddled until he convincingly shrieked his way into existence.' The list of his ailments during his lifetime is lengthy and included asthma, dropsy, gout, emphysema, manic depression, chronic bronchitis and a diseased bladder that made him incontinent. He eventually went blind in one eye and suffered aphasia.

He said of himself that, "My health hath seldom afforded me a single day of ease."

Yet, his achievements were colossal. The dictionary alone, although individual and quirky was a masterpiece of study and learning. At 75, he took to his bed, and it was clear his life would soon be at an end, but he refused to accept its imminence. While in bed, he continued to have intellectual discourse with his friends and late at night he was translating Greek poems into Latin (which were then published) up to a few weeks before his death. It seemed that even the approach of death itself could not abate his passion for learning. He had an amortal's changeless zest for life, throughout his life.

As far a choice of what to wear is concerned, the big difference between amortals and us ordinary mortals is that the least of their concerns is what others will think of their choice. Other things in their lives are far more important, unless, of course, their whole life has been about clothes. For amortal Vivienne Westwood, an outstanding businesswoman and the grand dame of dress designing, clothes have always been a passion. When she was 51, she was awarded an OBE by the Queen for services to fashion. On the day of the award, she twirled her skirts for the benefit of the press and revealed she was not wearing knickers, an event she considered highly amusing. She still, at 70, wears exotic styles that push forward the boundaries of fashion. She is not afraid to display beautifully crafted jewellery on her wrists, which does nothing to disguise the veins that stand out on the backs of her hands. If age has touched her, she does not seem to have noticed.

One difference between amortals such as Vivienne Westwood and ordinary mortals over 60 or 70 years of age, is that she has to attend occasions when she is expected to look resplendent, but for many older people, those occasions are few and far between. A friend of mine, an artist with an elegant figure, now in her 60s, was describing to me an exotic evening dress she coveted. All lace and sequins, it was reduced to a price she could have stretched to afford, but she didn't buy it. As she looked at her purse and then looked at the dress, a thought crossed her mind, *When would I wear it?*

In truth, there are fewer and fewer occasions in the lives of some of us when something really special is called for. Even a 90th birthday party amongst one's peers at a residential home is not quite the occasion for a sequinned dress, although perhaps it should be.

Should she have bought that dress? There are many people around, both of my age, and of course those who are younger, who are anxious to tell us to spruce ourselves up, to get our wig powdered or on the other hand to act our age. Our genes ensure that youth appears beautiful in the eyes of most people, because the future of the human race depends on men being attracted to women and women to men. So, the hunched shoulders, the thin bony legs, the bingo 'wings', the scraggy neck, the blotched thighs are the ugly signs of old age. In the past, they summoned up images of a witch, a crone or a hag, epitome of malice, bad temper and evil. The aged body is surely ugly compared to the smooth skinned, bronzed body of youth. But as the old saying goes, 'Beauty is in the eye of the beholder.' We have to accept that human cells, the living cells that make us what we are, are born to die and cannot always to be replaced, which has the remarkable result that our faces are a record of our life. An old adage runs, 'Beautiful young people are works of nature, but beautiful old people are works of art', and in some cultures, they see nothing but great beauty in the faces of their old people, perhaps because their attitude to their old people is so very different from ours; the old are not criticised but are admired because the young respect their experience and their wisdom.

A magazine by Age UK certainly shows very positive, even beautiful photographs, of the faces of the elderly, even though they too, I guess, may have been airbrushed. Airbrushing was unknown in the 17th and 18th centuries but artists produced some really outstanding portraits of old people. There is a portrait of an old peasant by Georges de la Tour[15] dated around 1618 and another by Hyacinthe Rigaud[16] of his mother, Marie Serre; both show the magnificence of old age. Then there is that of an 'Old Woman' by Francoise du Parc[17]. These show a beauty that has far greater depth than that of any young beauty Queen. Christian Seybold's 18 'Old Woman with Green Scarf' of 1795 is not only full of beauty but of character. You can see in her face her determined personality, the sorrow that at some time she appears to have suffered and the strength of will that seems to sustain her. She is dignified and magnificently beautiful. And it is not by chance the portrait's title mentions a rather beautiful green scarf.

Thinking back to my friend who wanted to buy an evening dress, what I should have said was, "Of course you should have bought that dress – and find an occasion to wear it."

Yet, when portrait painters represent a face, they do not paint what is, but what they see and interpret. When we look in a mirror at ourselves, the image we see is never the same as the image anyone else will see, as anyone knows who has tried to tell an anorexic that she is painfully thin.

As Anthony Gormly said, "We live on the other side of our appearance. Our faces belong more to others than ourselves."

For of course we focus on what we want to see or what we fear we will see. Many people, as they get older, spend less and less time looking in the mirror – they do not want to 'accept the transformation that makes our bodies ugly.' Marie de Hennezel[19] in *The Way of the Heart* suggests that we should instead forget ourselves and 'explore emotions such as joy.' She goes on to say we should 'stop looking at ourselves and instead see the world around us and the marvel of it.' It is good advice. I know when I look in the mirror my preoccupation is with stray ends of hair escaping the clip, about which I can do something; I really notice nothing else. I do not want to examine my scraggy neck or my crow's feet about which I can do nothing. Perhaps the knowledge, that is denied to all young people, except to those who at an early age have learned to come to terms with disfigurement, is something that is now patently obvious to us – it really doesn't matter! Jenny Joseph[20] summed it up beautifully in her poem 'Warning.'

When I am an old woman, I shall wear purple

With a red hat that doesn't go, and doesn't suit me.

It is not altogether helpful to put people into categories. It is like asking someone of mixed race whether they are black or white. When it comes to our attitude to clothes as we grow older, we are all individuals. Yet, I suggest that there are three broad categories. It could be said that for some people, choice of clothes or concern about appearance, for one reason or another, does not play an important part in their thinking. They dress as they have always done, and they dress for comfort. Others, whose self-esteem has always depended to a large extent upon the way they present themselves still enjoy shopping for clothes and will only go out if they are satisfied that they are looking their best. Perhaps the attitude of the former could be summed up by, 'When I am old, I will be the same he slob I was at 40', while the second group will be like my friend of 80. She walks with difficulty and has to rely on others for transport, but she will still go on a special expedition to buy a new hat and a matching shopping bag. A third group, the amortals, are so busy pursuing their dreams, they have no time to stop and wonder if they are dressing appropriately for their age.

So, as Carol Matthau said, "There is no old age. There is, as there always was, just you, and you will go on doing things the way you have always done them."

Do whatever pleases you. It is your life.

PS But just remember the words of Mary Quant, "The real rewarding thing about my age is that you don't have to take things quite so seriously. Most annoying is that other people do still take things seriously."

If that is your feeling too, take comfort. You are not a 'real' old person yet.

Chapter 7 Notes

1. Langer, Ellen, J, 2009, Counterclockwise, Ballantyne Books, New York
2. Gok Wan Clothes Show TV 4 in 2011
3. Tim Lott Observer article (02/01/11) p6
4. Miller, Jane, (2010) Crazy Age, Virago Press, London imprint of Little, Brown book grp
5. Clapp, Susannah, Observer article on Fanny Karst, "Granny takes a trip" 12/04/09
6. ibid
7. Botelho, Lynn A P (Thane, Pat, Editor) (2005) "The History of Old Age" 143 Thames and Hudson Ltd; London
8. Edna O'Brien Observer Interview by Rachel Cooke 06/02/11
9. Lisa Jardine Radio 4 Woman's Hour 2010
10. Eva Wiseman Observer 22/05/11 Life and Style – Up Front
11. Mayer, Catherine (2011), Amortality p12, Vermilion an imprint of Ebury Publishing, Random House Group, London
12. Hennezell, Marie de, 2011 (English Language Edition) The Warmth of the Heart, Rodale imprint of Pan Macmillan Publishers Ltd
13. Boswell, James, (1906) The Life of Samuel Johnson. Hutchinson & Co, London
14. ibid
15. The Long History of Old Age, page 149 George de la Tour

16. ibid page 147 Marie de Serre by her son Hyacinthe Rigaud
17. ibid page 200 Francoise du Parc, The Old Woman
18. ibid p 207 Christian Seybold's Woman with Green Scarf
19. Hennezell, Marie de (English Language Edition) (2011) The Warmth of the Heart, Rodale imprint of Pan Macmillan Publishers Ltd, London
20. Joseph, Jennifer and Pythian Ashton-Jewell, 1997, Poem Warning in Selected Poems, Bloodaxe, Souvenir Press Ltd, London

Chapter 8
The Generation Gap

Moke[1] was an elderly man. Although he lived with his tribe, the Mbuti pigmies, he had no wife and enjoyed a solitary life, often wandering into the bush with no apparent purpose in mind, or sometimes he would just sit on his own, doing nothing. People generally left him alone, but they recognised his great love for children, especially those who appeared to be rejected by the others, children who did not fit in.

One such a boy was Kaoya. That was his real name, but the Mbuti nearly always called their children by a nickname and Kaoya was always known as Ibambi. Kaoya knew exactly why he was called that. Ibambi was a soft round fruit that would often fall to the ground with an unexpected plop that made people jump. Ibambi was clumsy and often tripped and fell, so he was not happy with his nickname, especially when he fell over. Then everyone clapped their hands under their armpits, making an echoey plopping noise and they shouted, "An Ibambi fruit has fallen. Did you hear that?"

He often responded by acting the fool, rolling on the ground like a fruit rolling downhill, while the children shouted and rushed round in circles, as if looking for the fruit and then falling on top of Ibambi with great peals of laughter. At other times, he would show how upset he was at being made to look so foolish and he protested about his nickname. So, they gave him another, 'Hanakiri', which means, 'he who has no brains.' That was worse. Better to stick with Ibambi, and it stayed with him throughout his childhood.

When he was about eight years old, the childish nickname became more and more hurtful. The adults understood and used only his real name. He began spending more time with them than with the other boys, which was not acceptable in Mbuti society. His mother was angry with him and warned him that if he did not go back and spend his days with the boys in the bobi, the boys' house, she would send to him to play with the girls in the elima, the girls' house. Ibambi was in tears. It was something beyond his comprehension. Was his mother telling him he was a girl? The only person who would be able to explain it to him was old Moke. He ran to Moke and grabbed him by the waist and looked up at him, "I'm not a girl, am I, Moke?"

Moke looked grave and held him at arm's length, looking at him intently. Then he felt his chest. "Well, you are not like any girl I have ever seen!" he said, and they both giggled and laughed and walked off into the bush together.

But this is not the end of the story. This incident between old Moke and Ibambi did not solve Ibambi's problems. His feeling that he was an outsider persisted. He felt rejected by the 'gang' and rejected by his mother. His attempt to find a solution has little parallel in western culture, although had he been older and living in the west, I suppose he might have sought to find a girlfriend to confide in. In Mbuti society, moving from childhood to adulthood followed a traditional procedure. When boys and girls came up to puberty and they wished to show their intention to go through the next initiation ceremony, which might be one or two years away, they would engage in dancing together. The girls had with them light whips with which they would attack a boy they favoured, signalling that they wished him to come and sleep with them.

Ibambi determined to join the dancing. He would prove he was a boy ready for manhood and with great bravado, he joined in. The boys were not at all bothered but the girls were amused and determined to have fun at the expense of a boy who was hardly of any age to offer them any satisfaction. They surrounded him, dancing in a circle merrily brandishing their whips, playfully whipping each other.

"Go home," they sang, "and dance with yourself. Go home!"

In their language, the word for dance is also the word for 'play' and the word for 'sex.'

Ibambi was beside himself with rage and embarrassment. His mother looking on, mortified for him as well as for herself, grabbed at him, bodily lifting him off the ground, as if he were a baby. In floods of tears, he rushed into their hut and scattered the fire, where their food was cooking. Then picking up a stick which he threw at his mother, he ran to the far end of the camp into the arms of old Moke, who had silently watched it all from a distance.

Did old Moke cuddle him in his arms and explain that really it was quite a stupid thing to do and that his mother only pulled him away because she loved him? Did he assure him as any sensible parent would, that in a few years' time, of course he would be ready to join the dance of the boys and girls before their initiation? He did none of those things. This was not the time for logic, for talking rationally, for appealing to common sense. Emotional understanding does not come through logic, but through the emotions and the Mbuti express their emotions, as do teenagers everywhere, through song and dance.

Moke grabbed Ibambi, ignoring his tears, and started to dance with him, creating a catchy jingle, "Ba bi na kali, zu bi ekadi," which played on the similar sound of bi na kali and bi ekadi.

THEY are dancing with the girls; WE are dancing as one.

Soon, Ibambi joined in the song and as the Mbuti do, as today's rappers do, they played with the words and with their mispronunciation of kali (girls) made it sound quite ridiculous. But the word ekadi, which means unity, love, togetherness, they always sang meaningfully and with seriousness. They invented new jingles,

Like elephants they crash (the boys)
Like antelopes we leap
Like witches their noise (the girls)
But we sing with joy

When ideas for new lyrics ran out, Moke became more excited and even more inventive. He took off his raffia hat and they danced together with that. The two really became as one. The old and the young celebrating how much each meant to the other is so often known instinctively, but in western society, it so often goes unspoken.

Then old Moke picked up a large leaf, throwing it into the air and letting it fall like rain; they danced with a flower that dripped with water; and then Ibambi dropped to the ground, plonk! Like an Ibambi fruit. The song and the dance were infectious; those looking on started to dance too, celebrating the oneness of the old with the young, the men with the women, the tribe with the creatures and the fruits of the forest; as Colin Turnbull says of it, "A true dance of atonement."

Suddenly, Moke stopped and grabbed at Ibambi. "Look," he said, and pointed at Ibambi's mother. "What is she doing?"

His mother was dancing with another woman, who was crouching low down, as if she were a child. Ibambi looked at them and then paused. Suddenly, he knew what she was telling him. He sang louder than ever,

She is dancing with a child! She is dancing with me!

There are times when words that should be spoken are left unsaid, but there are also times when there is no need for words. The story surely resonates throughout the world in many, many cultures. Old people are somehow able to identify with the needs of the young, to have a common understanding. Perhaps it is because the young and the old are outside the perimeter of decision making and they make common cause in their powerlessness. Or perhaps it is as Turnbull suggests they are nearer to non-existence, the time before birth and after death. Whatever the reason, this is the relationship we want to see, yes expect to see, between young and old. It is a relationship that appears to be almost universal.

Something that has puzzled scientists for a long time is the fact that the human species is one of the very few among mammals where once the female experiences the end of her fertility, the menopause, she does not die, but may live some 30% of her life in her post-fertile period.

Conversely, the male continues to produce sperm to a very great age. What evolutionary purpose does this serve? We all know of men who have become fathers beyond the age of 70. Charlie Chaplin's last child was born when he was 74. Des O'Connor fathered a child at 72. The oldest father alive at present is Jamjit Ramjav, who had a child at 94. The mother was in her 50s and had a normal delivery. He drinks 3.5 quarts of milk a day, eats a pound of almonds and a pound of ghee (clarified butter) and likes sex three times a night, none of which I guess explains anything.

To explain the menopause, some geneticists have produced the 'grandmother hypothesis' [2], which proposes that when our ancestors were still hunter-gatherers, and much of the hard work such as the digging of tubers was done by the women of childbearing age, it became an advantage to have older women who were no longer capable of childbearing to help with the care and rearing of her grandchildren. It enabled more offspring to survive and was therefore an evolutionary advantage.

This theory is much disputed, and the fact that grandparents, especially grandmothers, have a close attachment to their grandchildren does not have to be explained by evolutionary theory.

As Charles and Ann Morse have said, "A child needs a grandparent, anybody's grandparent, to grow a little more securely into an unfamiliar world."[3]

Jean Giles-Sims, PhD Professor of Sociology [4] tells a typical story of a modern a grandmother, living in New England, who had a 12-year-old grandson living many miles away in New Jersey. She was still working full time, but she remembered how she had baked pies with her own grandmother, how they had sewed doll's clothes together. It was not what she had done with her grandmother that was important but that they had had a loving relationship that had given her a feeling of self-worth and of security that had lasted her a lifetime. Knowing that her grandson was home alone after school and having mastered the computer as part of her job, the answer was simple. She now connects with him almost daily with talk about how things have gone at school. She can bring to bear her own experience of the difficulties of coping with the hated maths homework or the cruelty of so-called 'friends.'

This type of relationship has spawned many quotes which idolise the state of being a grandparent: 'Grandmas are Moms with lots of frosting.'

'Perfect love does not come until the first grandchild.'

'A house needs a grandma in it.' (Louisa May Alcott)

'Grandmas never run out of hugs or cookies.'

Most of us know that not all grandparents can live up to this idolised version of being a grandparent, and grandchildren too know that grandparents are not perfect.

I remember the only grandparent I really knew, my mother's mother, with great fondness. I recall sitting at her knee and learning what a faith in an all loving and all protecting God meant in a person's life. She lived with us at that time and to me she was the storybook grandmother – except she had one memorable fault. She was keen to make sure we got enough vitamins, so before dinner every day she made us drink a cup of the hot water that the cabbage had been cooked in because, 'it is good for you.' We did not agree but she was probably right as the cabbage had been cooked in a large saucepan of water for at least an hour.

She was a Seventh Day Adventist, having been converted in her 50s, I guess, and I still have her bible containing all the ribbons she received for reading the bible daily and attending church weekly. At the time of her conversion, she ran a small shop in the east end of London. Her sailor husband returned from time to time and regularly emptied the till of all its money to go drinking. Converting to a church that insisted that no work should be done from sunset on Friday to sunset on Saturday, she closed her shop on the busiest day of the week. Her commitment was total.

It was her commitment that eventually became the greatest barrier between her and my parents, and her commitment failed to make me into a lifelong believer in her church or any other. In the family she was known as the 'Little Queen Victoria' because of her authoritarian attitude, which eventually led to her leaving our home and living on her own for most of the rest of her life. It was not just her infuriating refusal to allow us to listen to the wireless (it was still the wireless in the 30s) on a Saturday, but because that was symptomatic of her dominance over the household. My father could not tolerate it. I still remember her though with great admiration and affection. She did much for me, not least in making me think for myself and believe in myself, flawed character though she was.

Barack Obama, former president of the most powerful country in the world demonstrated his love for his grandmother in a very public way. She had become seriously ill during the presidential campaign and became worse towards the date of the election. 14 days before the country was due to go to the poles, to the dismay of the Democratic Party, he made an unprecedented decision to leave the campaign trail and travel to Hawaii to see her. The election was not a foregone conclusion and every day of the campaign was vital. Once it was over, win or lose, he could have spared the time to visit her, but despite what he had been told, he had a premonition that her time was up.

Against all advice, he lost two days campaigning, and flew to Honolulu. After a number of short visits to her apartment, reluctantly he returned to the work in hand. It was a decision he never regretted.

Obama was born of mixed-race parents. His mother's parents came from the Midwest, from Kansas; they were of European stock, that had fought on the anti-slave Unionist side in the Civil War. So they were liberal with regard to race, but even so, it must have been something of a shock to them when their daughter Ann announced she intended to marry a black African from Kenya, one of the elders of the Luo tribe. Perhaps it was easier because by that time they had moved to Hawaii, a racial melting pot, but Obama offers no record of what they really thought.

The young Barack was unaware of the implications of being of mixed race and his grandfather, 'Gramps', mixed socially and in business with all comers, irrespective of the colour of their skin. Neither had the young Barack reason to believe his beloved Toots (Tutu, the Hawaii word for grandmother, was shortened to Toots) was racially prejudiced. From the time he was born until he left Hawaii for America when he was nineteen, there were only a few years when he was not living either with his grandparents or close by.

He said, "She's the one who taught me about hard work... She's the one who put off buying a new car or a new dress for herself so that I could have a better life." She meant as much to him as his own mother.

It was when his mother remarried and went to live with her new husband in Indonesia, that Barack suddenly awoke to the implications of being 'black.' He was nine and sitting in his mother's office, when he came across a picture in a 'Life' magazine that shocked him to the core and sent sweat coursing down his face. As he said later, it was like being ambushed. It was the eerie picture of a black man that had undergone treatment to try and pass himself off as white. The treatment had failed, and he looked like the victim of some radiation accident. Barack learned that 100s of black people in America were trying this same treatment to cast off their blackness and to become whites. Was this what being black meant?

The sudden revelation that the world contained blacks and whites and that their expectations were not the same haunted him throughout his teenage years and beyond. It raised questions about his own identity as he slowly discovered that blacks could be as racist as whites, even in a multicultural society such as that of Hawaii.

It was a few years later, back in Hawaii, that his confidence was once more shaken to the core. He discovered that racism existed not only amongst his school contemporaries, but it existed in his own family – in his beloved grandmother. The incident occurred one day when Toots and Gramps were having a 'tiff', something which was a part of their daily lives and which always ended in compromise. Toots worked for a local bank and she had worked her way up to be the first woman vice president as a result of dedication to her job. She always arrived there early, before everyone else, waking at five in the morning and setting off on the 6:30 am bus. One day, she was accosted by a large man at the bus stop demanding money, a not infrequent occurrence in a city where there were many poor vagrants. It worried her and she asked Gramps if he would take her to work in the car the next day, which meant he would have to get up much earlier than he liked; but it was not that that created the outburst.

"But!" in explanation, she shrieked, "He was black!"

When the young Barack came from his bedroom to see what was happening, Toots retreated.

"What is the matter with her?" his grandfather shouted. "She's only bothered because he was black!" and then he stopped, taken aback at the sight of his black grandson.

Barack was devastated. The only person he could think of talking to was a black poet who lived in a broken-down shack on the other side of town, a man who spent most of his time in the kitchen drinking whiskey with a book of poetry on his knee. He had often been taken to see Frank by Gramps, who spent hours with him sitting and talking, sitting and drinking, or just sitting. It was three years since Barack's last visit but Frank needed no encouragement to talk about what it meant to be black.

"Your grandfather's a good man," he said, "But he doesn't know me. Your grandfather will never know what (being black) feels like."

Sometime later, when Barack went to college in California, one other comment came back to his mind, 'They'll give you a corner office and invite you to fancy dinners and tell you that you are a credit to your race. Until you actually start running things and then they'll yank on your chain and let you know you that maybe a well-trained well-paid nigger, but you're a nigger just the same.'

Was it that conversation with Frank, which he never forgot, that determined Obama to prove him wrong? But was it also the determination that he had learned from Toots that helped him to prove it?

The row between his grandmother and grandfather that day was just one more event that led Barack towards understanding how deeply history had ingrained in white people an assumption of their superiority. He realised that white people, as well as black were at the mercy of the past. He felt no anger, only sadness, and at that time, incomprehension.

He said years later as she lay seriously ill, "She poured everything she had into me."

Toots never lived long enough to see him become President of the United States. She died the day before the election.

It does not matter whether you are a Moke – a grandparent by proxy or a Toots, a genetic grandparent – the relationship can be just as strong. There must be many who remember a spinster schoolteacher who became a surrogate grandmother to her children. You do not have to be anyone with special virtues, and you do not even have to try; you just have to be 'old' in the eyes of the young. You just have to be there. That is the virtue of the old. They do not have to 'do' anything.

They just have to 'be.'

It is not always so. Turn over the page and there's quite a different picture.

The first line in an article in the Observer[6] reads, 'Grandparents are rebelling.' It seems that a grandmother has set up a website for Grannies (*grannynet.co.uk*, not to be confused with *gransnet.co.uk*), but it is not a site to exchange cosy stories about their delightful young grandchildren, but the discovery that grannies need to get together to stand firm against the demands of their daughters and their daughters-in-law. Grannies are younger and fitter than they were in the past and their lives are no longer centred on the family's needs but on their own. So they are in a dilemma when they see the demands being made of them for childcare. By setting up the website, Lorna Edwards[7], the founder, says, "We hope to get a clear picture of what today's grandparents think is and is not acceptable when it comes to childcare."

So, what is it that grandparents are worried about and for which it was found necessary to draw up a charter to be signed by parent and grandparent? There is a page of questions and points for discussion, each followed by the signatures of both parties on the following topics: How many days/hours a week does each party think acceptable? To pay or not to pay? Your place or mine? Who provides/pays for the equipment? What about food? Who decides the rules of discipline?

Where you have rules, you normally have to have sanctions for breaking them.

"You forgot to send Jenny with her Barbie doll, so I had to buy her a new one. That will be $25, plus a fine of $5."

In our society, no one teaches you how to become a grandparent. Mistakes and misunderstandings are inevitable, but this seems to be a very bizarre way of dealing with the grandparent-parent relationship.

Of course, problems that arise in families from time to time cause tension and arguments and they are all questions to which answers have to be established by mutual agreement or sometimes by becoming a permanent cause for grumbling, if not a family row.

However, it is difficult to see how by sitting down in conference and going through these questions, line by line, deciding on agreed answers and then each putting a signature to the agreed decisions – assuming they do come to some agreement – is likely avoid future arguments.

The problem is that this is not a question of calm logical thinking that is able to produce the 'right' practical answers. What you can afford to buy for your grandchildren is a practical question. What you would like to buy for your grandchildren is a question of emotion. As the Observer newspaper article points out, the problem arises only because what you want to do for yourself conflicts with what you feel you ought to do for them. To pretend that by signing a document you can absolve yourself of the feeling of guilt that you really ought to be doing more, but then you have your own life to lead, is not the answer. 'Grandparents demand their charter of rights' is a headline we could do without.

The dilemma is a real one, but it is one the answer to which only the individual can decide. It depends on material circumstances, geographical distance, the needs of the grandchildren and their parents, and above all, the relationship between grandparent and parent (the grandparent's own offspring), already established since the day the parent was born. Each has to judge whether the sacrifice of giving up time and money for their grandchildren is worth the rewards they get in return.

The rewards of being a grandparent may be as important as the rewards of being a parent. Professor Ann Buchanan[8], director of the Centre for Research into Parenting and Children in the Department of Social Policy and Social Work at Oxford University questioned more than 1500 children and teenagers who had been cared for by grandparents. As a result of this research, she said, "What was especially interesting was the link between involved grandparents and adolescent well-being. In short, children grow up happier if their grandparents are involved in their upbringing."

I notice that the grannynet website has now moved on and much of the content consists of a plethora of advertisements for things to buy in the grannynet shop and stories about the unexpected and delightful behaviour of their young charges.

There is less of, 'If I were paid as a carer, I could earn £400,' and more of, 'My grandchild's always saying cute things.' The other day she said, ' Look Nana, pussy's doing an upside-down belly,' or, ' When I asked my noisy granddaughter to find the button to turn the volume down on the radio, she pulled up her skirt and showed me her belly button.'

That development on this website I think was inevitable, because whatever the culture, whatever the time in history, whatever the personal story, a bond between grandparents and grandchildren appears to be the natural order of things.

But all this leaves out the other actor in the story, the parent, the parent of the grandchild, the grown-up child of the grandparent, the piggy in the middle. Some feel as though they stand in the middle, as in the children's game, with the grandparent calling the shots from one end and the grandchildren taking control at the other. The piggy in the middle is constantly looking from one to the other to see where they are going to throw the ball. What did the mum of the 12-year-old think about her own mum in New England connecting daily on the computer with him after school? Was she pleased or annoyed at grandma's intrusion? Did she feel guilty because she could not be home for her son? Was she jealous of her son's relationship with his grandmother? Was she relieved because she could be sure of what he was doing when he came home from school? Was she furious because grandma was encouraging the boy to spend too much time on the computer?

On another website, *forparentsbyparents.com*, you find comments like, 'I am finding it hard now to cope with the unnecessary daily intrusion of my father. He rings every morning and afternoon to talk to my son. He has nothing new to say. I cannot get him to back off and let us alone.'

Another angrily says to her mum (now the grandmother), 'Do you remember how you used to grumble to us as children about your mother being an interfering know-it-all? Well, you should!'

A mother of a 6 and 4-year-old says, 'My mother-in-law has been very involved in raising them from day one. At first, I found this a terrible intrusion. My mum-in-law would come into the house whilst baby and I were asleep and clean up for me, which I took as a slur on my ability to cope.' But she goes on to say, 'It took me a long time to realise the benefits of allowing grandparents to help…they have far more patience and experience… I believe my kids are kinder and calmer because of her input.'

The truth is, in western society, the pig-in-the-middle is not an accurate analogy, for in this case it is the pig-in-the-middle that usually has the ball. It is the parent and not the grandparent or the child that has the power. Power lies with the economic providers in our society and this is enshrined in our cultural mores. The ten commandments require you to 'honour your father and mother', but not to obey them. Whether or not the parents use that power is up to them, but society as a whole will sanction their right to decide how far they accede to the will of their parents (the grandparents) and how they will exert control over their children. How they use that right is vitally important and is constrained by social, moral and emotional considerations. This is not true in those societies where the elders were (or in a few societies still are) at the top of the social hierarchy and whose opinions had to be listened to.

The term 'ageism' was apparently coined by Robert Neil Butler in 1968, but it formalised attitudes in western society that go back far longer than that. It recognised not simply that older people had different physical attributes from those who are younger – they cannot run as fast, their skin cells do not replace themselves so perfectly, they are more prone to disease, but that there was also some adverse prejudice involved. They are relegated to the backburner. Yet that prejudice should be balanced, as we have seen by a much more positive agreement that older people still have much to offer. Moving from being a child to becoming an adolescent and then to becoming a parent all require adjustment, sometimes slow, sometimes quite precipitous. There is always a reluctance to accept that the years are slipping by and that realisation may come at any age. It may be just as hard for a footballer to give up his job at 40 as it is for an accountant to retire at 60. But while no one is surprised if the footballer turns to a new career, at 60 ageism writes people off as if our society no longer needed them. It is a healthier society that treats them with respect and welcomes what they have to offer.

Things are changing and in the 21st century and perhaps for the first time ever in the west, it is the older generation that has economic security, which gives them much more power to say no to the parents of their grandchildren, to insist on their way of doing things, to criticise and to choose when, where and how they will give help. Grandparents are indeed rebelling. Their numbers too are increasing and will continue to increase. There is a monumental change in balance. By 2030, 25% of the population in the UK will be over 65, which means 25% of the country's voters, and as the proportion of older people who vote, is greater than the proportion of younger people; politicians will have to listen to their pensioners.

Perhaps, just perhaps, ageism is not here to last, and a cultural change will overturn attitudes that have persisted in the west for 3000 years.

Chapter 8 Notes

1. Turnbull, Colin, M, The Human Cycle 1983, Jonathan Cape Ltd London
2. Dawkin, Richard, (1976). The selfish gene. Oxford: Oxford University Press.
3. Morse, Charles and Ann from www.finestquotes.com
4. Giles-Sims, Jean (grandmotherconnections.com)
5. Obama, Barack, (2004) Dreams from my Father, Crown Publishers, Random House Inc, New York
6. Hill, Amelia Observer 24/08/08
7. Edwards, Lorna, www.grannynet.co.uk
8. Buchanan, Ann, from current normative study of grandparents as seen through the eyes of young people. Ann Buchanan Ph.D., M.A. (Oxon.), CQSW is Director for the Oxford Centre for Research into Parenting and Children.

Facts to Ponder

The world's youngest grandmother is Romanian Rifca Stanescu, who became a grandmother at 23, when her daughter became a mother at 11.

There are 14 million grandparents in the UK, half of whom are under 65.

A third of UK grandparents spend an average of three days a week caring for grandchildren. An estimated 50% of children in urban China are cared for by grandparents

In Sweden, grandparents can take time off work to look after grandchildren. National Grandparents Day has been celebrated in the US since 1978.

Chapter 9
Alone or Lonely

Autophobia – fear of being alone, by oneself

I'm the one that's got to die when it's time for me to die, so let me live my life the way I want to.

– Jimi Hendrix, Jimi Hendrix – Axis: Bold as Love

LONELY WOMAN DIES AFTER 2 DAYS LYING ON A STONE FLAGGED FLOOR

Her shouts for help went unheard as she lay for two days on the cold stone floor in the hall of her cottage. 80 years old and living alone she had fallen and try as she may, she could not get back on her feet. A caller eventually found her, and she was rushed to hospital, but she died the next day of pneumonia.

This actually happened, exactly like that, but this piece never appeared in a newspaper, as no journalist got wind of it. It is just the sort of story that attracts our attention, enlists our sympathy, arouses our concern and gnaws at our conscience. It is just the sort of story that is manna to the journalist. All her friends were so relieved that no newspaperman ever heard about this piece of drama.

But what is the truth behind it? Certainly, there are lonely people who die every day in tragic circumstances and whose death may not be discovered for days, weeks or months. It is almost unbelievable that such things can happen in the 21st century, in our supposedly civilised country. And it strikes at our hearts.

Humans are not the only animals that show emotion at the death of another. It occurs in many species; from greylag geese, who hang their heads when a mate dies; to sealions, who wail pitifully should one of their young become the victim of a killer whale. Many others are aware of loss and maybe even the tragedy of unexpected loss. Elephants show great concern when one of their group is killed.

Cynthia Moss describes the actions of the members of an elephant family after a group member had been shot, 'Teresa and Trista became frantic and knelt down and tried to lift her up. They worked their tusks under her back and under her head. At one point, they succeeded in lifting her into a sitting position, but her body flopped back down. Her family tried everything to rouse her, kicking and tusking her, and Tullulah even went off and collected a trunkful of grass and tried to stuff it in her mouth.'[1]

The human emotion felt at the death of another is, I suspect, far more complex. For an animal, perhaps it is just the loss itself, the feeling of emptiness, the inevitable change in the daily routine because they, like us, are social animals and all their activities are bound up with others in the group. Humans, however, are able to enter into the emotions of others and to recreate the feelings we believe others undergo in desperate situations.

Yet, there is a danger in this. We wince at the idea of someone living alone and dying alone, fearful that someone somewhere has neglected a duty. Someone must be to blame. When it happens in our own society, the guilt rubs off on ourselves; but too often we create stereotypes, and our real understanding of the situation may be wide of the mark. The story of Janet, we shall call her Janet, the lady who died because of a fall outlined in the newspaper headlines above, is the story of a tragic life, but it could be that she, looking down from wherever she now resides would not have seen her death as tragic; perhaps a little unfortunate, but perhaps even timely.

Should society do more to prevent sad events such as these? Beyond childhood, we are encouraged to take responsibility for our own actions and we delight in the opportunity to do so. Most of us want to decide to have the right to decide where we will live, what job we will take, how we conduct our lives. In old age, unless we ask for help, the cruelty of taking that 'right' away from us is perhaps something that younger people cannot begin to understand. Of course, if we become mentally or physically incapable of making those choices, that is another matter, but many old people make a conscious decision to live on their own and I believe they have every right to do so.

In her old age, Janet had considered moving to live in a town near one of her sons, but certainly not with him. 'Friends' wanted to persuade her to live in sheltered accommodation in a town, where she knew a number of people. The social services offered to keep an eye on her. She had considered all of these options and rejected them. She rejected them, in spite of the risks she knew she was taking and the lack of comfort in her home. There was no central heating, just electric fires. There was not even hot water. She lived on microwave meals, straight from the cartons, which were piled two feet high on the kitchen floor. Staying with a friend after a car accident, she fell and it took two people to get her onto her feet, but as soon as she was well enough, she insisted on going back to her own house, knowing the risk of falling again. Mentally alert (she had a computer and apparently enjoyed using it), she made the decision to stay, consciously and with full knowledge of the possible consequences. It was that spirit of independence, that was more important to her than anything else, and that had brought her through a difficult life. Without that, she would never have reached the age of 80. Without that, she would have had no reason to live.

Many of the events that marked Janet's life were not just difficult but tragic. Her mother died soon after she was born; her father hated her because she was a girl and not a boy, registering her birth as that of a boy; she was fostered by an unforgiving aunt who resented the task imposed on her. As a young girl, she escaped a murderous paedophile, which left an indelible dent in her ability to trust anyone. Although she eventually married, her husband took up with another woman. She finally found herself in a cottage five miles from the nearest shop, without being able to drive a car and knowing no one in the village. It was the lowest point in her life.

It was there that she lived, on her own for the next 30 years and she appeared to live there happily. She had many acquaintances who loved her lively personality, her jokes and her pertinent observations. She would chuckle to see a cow moving her head over a gate, seemingly wanting a conversation. She was an excellent mimic and had once enjoyed an acting career, but she never had any real friends. It appears that she surrounded herself with an impenetrable shield because she dare not open herself up to the possibility of further hurt.

Although she went shopping regularly and met up with friends for coffee or accepted their hospitality for lunch, she never invited anyone into her own home. In later years, it was almost impossible to get inside her house as she had become an obsessive hoarder. She threw nothing away and in every room including her bedroom and kitchen you could only cross the floor through a narrow passage of piled high boxes, papers, clothes, empty ready meal cartons, black bin bags, books, unemptied shopping bags and more. She had quarrelled with her near neighbours, as she did with most people eventually.

Was she lonely? I do not think so. She had conquered that demon long ago. She had established a satisfying daily routine. She noted down in the Radio Times all the programmes she wanted to hear or watch. She went shopping twice a week in the nearest town. Her life was structured. Was she happy? What does 'happy' mean in the context of her life? Who knows what her innermost feelings were? I guess she was as happy as she had ever been, but the truth was her secret.

She had learnt what it means to be really independent of other people. She knew that if she fell over alone in her house, she would have great difficulty in getting to her feet, because she was so overweight, caused as she knew herself too well, by her addiction to sweets and chocolate. When she did fall on that fateful day, she knew it was unlikely anyone would come to help her until the taxi man, who was due to come two days later to take her shopping. She would be annoyed, but unlike most of the rest of us, I am sure she would be resigned. She had come through so many disasters in her life (including a serious car accident just two years before when she broke her neck) that there would have been no panic. When the taxi man did arrive, he shouted through the letterbox, "Are you all right?"

The answer was not a pitiful moan or even a muted cry for help. "Of course I'm not all right," she shouted angrily.

In the hospital a day later, she was in great pain. That evening, she had a phone call from her son. Nothing could have given her more pleasure. She died an hour or so later. She was a survivor to the end. She showed if anyone could, how the human spirit can overcome a life of tragedy and she remained in charge of her life to the end.

Had Janet been persuaded against her will to go into a retirement home, how long would she have lived? It might have been for a longer or a much shorter time, we cannot tell. What I think is almost certain is that she would have become an empty shell – a car without an engine, a windmill without its sails, a boiler without fuel. Her death would have been a quiet, non-event – but of course, socially acceptable.

About 40% of old people consult their GP at some time or other about a mental health problem. That figure rises to 50% of those in hospital, while for those in residential homes the figure rises to 60%. 2 This should not be a surprise.

There is the story of Marie, a 72-year-old widow living alone in the Bronx, New York, many miles from her two grown up children and their families. She had arthritis, which made getting about difficult and the very busy streets, especially the trucks, made her nervous about going out. At night, it was the fear of crime, although in recent years crime rates are far lower than they were. She had no close friends living nearby and life for her became unbearable. Her only dream was to move, but as she said, "Where would I go? I can't afford to live anywhere else."3.

Life in old age was for her an insoluble problem.

By contrast, a retired police officer, John, aged 70, who lived with his wife in New York, was very active in the community. He volunteered to help programmes to help frail elderly people and children at risk. He was on the board of directors of several community organisations. With his wife, he visited shows on Broadway and frequently visited shops and museums. In his words, "(Brooklyn) is the perfect place to grow old."

Had John read wise books on preparation for old age and taken the advice to heart? I doubt it. The difference in attitude I would guess is more to do with personality, education, life's experience, and yes, probably finance. Health too plays a part, not so much actual disability as the perception of the limitations of ill health. Losing one's ability to hear must be the most traumatic of all disabilities for one whose life has been music and composing. Yet, this happened to Beethoven. He records the utter despair this brought about, and then although totally deaf, he went on to compose the Ninth Symphony and his last stirring quartets, some of his most remarkable and innovative works.

Matisse the great French artist and friend of Picasso had, in later life, an operation after which he had to use a wheelchair, or he was confined to his bed, which he had mounted on wheels. The exciting canvasses which he had once painted, and which had caused such a sensation in the art world were no longer possible. He changed his technique. He turned to cutting out pieces of coloured cardboard, which he used for amazing collages. His sense of colour and shape, which he had developed over many years, enabled him to produce creations that were simple and yet wonderfully imaginative, direct and compelling.

Few of us can expect to have the talents of Picasso or of Beethoven, but their determination to use their lives fruitfully stems from the same source as that of John the ex-policeman, who simply had administrative skills to offer; or of The Woman of Varnassi (see chapter2), who simply became a symbol by her very presence at a certain time in a certain place. Who can be lonely while still contributing to the life of a neighbour, a friend, the family or the wider world?

For many people, however, loneliness is a major curse. Take the headline in a modern popular magazine. It reads, *I FEEL SO ALONE*. Who is the article about – an old woman left to die in a high rise flat? No! This was Cheryl Cole, a fashion icon, a member of the hugely successful girl band, 'Girls Aloud' and a judge on *The X Factor*. It appears that she is scared of living on her own and her mum refused to move in.

AGE UK, a major charity, which does invaluable work in helping the elderly, is not above cashing in on the popular perception of the needs of old people. Together with a picture of a cheerful old lady (a model), one of their leaflets says, 'I know lots of people see me at the window. They probably think I am being nosey. A curtain twitcher. But I'm stuck in here because I can't go out there. And no one really visits me. Unless you count the milkman, but he comes before I am out of bed. I try not to get up too early. It only makes the day last longer. Which means more of the same. More of nothing.'

In smaller print over the page, you find, 'This leaflet contains a composite case study…it does not reflect the specific circumstances of any one person.'

Of course, there is nothing wrong with this approach. There are indeed people who need the help of AGE UK and who need it desperately and it is necessary to paint a one-sided stereotypical picture to enlist sympathy and financial help. The only concern is the effect it might have on people much younger when they consider their own old age and what it will mean for them.

Who are these old people who are really lonely and is it something that we should all fear, even expect as almost inevitable?

Loneliness in old age may be the result of poor health or lack of confidence, but most of all, it is likely to be because of poverty. Well-educated people of even moderate means are able to overcome loneliness, if they so wish, even when loss of hearing or sight, loss of mobility or chronic illness force changes in their lifestyle. On the other hand, given the opportunity to meet the 'curtain twitcher', we would find that she is likely to have little in common with the smiling model in the pamphlet with her perfect teeth, her discreet make-up, her well-groomed hair and designer glasses. She is far more likely to look haggard or aggressive, with grey depressions below her eyes, with a skinny neck and hair unkempt or hidden from view in a scarf. She may well be timid and unresponsive or perhaps argumentative and aggressive. It will be difficult to make her smile. Her room may show she is trying fairly unsuccessfully with its well-worn chair coverings and faded curtains to keep up appearances or it may show she has given that up altogether. This is the loneliness of poverty; fate having dealt her a bad hand. She is unlikely to have learned any social graces at school; she is likely to have felt useless at learning; and she will have coped with the world with aggression or retreat, both signs of a lack of confidence, a lack of self-esteem. Some of this may be genetic, some of it upbringing, but either way she has never 'made her way up in the world', perhaps even failing in her family relationships. Unless we have the compassion shown by the workers of AGE UK, she is not the kind of person whose photo on a leaflet is likely to enlist our help or that we would be even happy to meet.

It comes as no surprise that those at the lowest income level are the people most likely to be unhappy and dissatisfied with their lives at whatever age. The European Centre for Social Welfare, Policy and Research undertook a survey in 2009 in 30 countries of Europe 4 in an attempt to quantify the satisfaction of people at various ages at various income levels. The results confirmed this expectation. The poorer you are, the least satisfied you are with your life. However, on the whole, it was not those who were poor and old who hit rock bottom in the satisfaction stakes, it was the poor aged between 40 and 49, when perhaps many of them had not yet lost their partner and may even still have had children living with them. The low ebb of dissatisfaction comes not at the end of their lives. By the time they have reached 60, on average, people say they are at least as satisfied with their lives as they were in their teens and early twenties.

Comparing this with the happiness of people on average incomes comes another surprise. It appears that those people living in western Europe aged 30 to 50 and enjoying a life unencumbered by any real worries about money and enjoying a standard of living far above that in the rest of the world (apart from the USA) are more miserable and less satisfied with their lives than those who are elderly and poor. The graphs show that in all income groups, people are unhappiest during middle age. This is the U-Bend theory. Life's journey is uphill all the way to middle-age, when the road turns a corner, and from then on it is a downhill ride.

Many reasons have been put forward to explain this somewhat unexpected result. Perhaps it is because unhappy people die young or their grown-up family moving away causes distress, but if there is one reason that should give hope to those going through mid-life depression, it is that old age is something to look forward to. Similar types of survey undertaken in the USA show the same trends and one in particular[5] (see graph at the end of the chapter) shows that the feeling of well-being continues to rise inexorably beyond the age of 65 and is greater than that felt at the age of 18!

This is confirmed by a small group of my friends, all in their 70s and 80s, some of whom live on their own and all of whom have arthritis, failing hearing or failing sight or unexplained pains, but all of whom are remarkably and determinedly cheerful. They seldom mention their aches and pains and pass them off. When asked how they are they are likely to say, 'Not so bad', or 'What can I expect at my time of life!' They are far more likely to talk about the joyous pleasures of programming their own day or enjoying naughty treats. One of them loves Toblerone and she is conscious that it may not be good for your health, so she cuts off a single triangle and divides that into three, one to have with coffee in the morning, one for mid-afternoon and the other when she is sitting quietly in the evening watching television. She has another secret. Hidden in her drawer is a Mars bar! If she really cannot wait until her next session with the Toblerone, she knows she can always dive into the Mars bar.

Having passed the time of no going back, when there is no possibility of convincing yourself that you are years younger than you feel or than you look, with only old age and eventual death to look forward to, it is obvious as it never was before, that the present is all important. It is a lesson few people learn when they are young unless they are a Buddhist monk or a poet. So although you know that eating a Mars bar or smoking another cigarette may well shorten your life (so they tell you), what sort of life will that be without those things that make it most pleasurable for you? The Toblerone salves my friend's conscience; the thought of the Mars bar makes life worth living.

This explanation for the unexpected contentment that old age often brings is supported by theories based on research. Laura Carstensen, of Stanford University, suggests that because old people are closer to death, they focus more on things that are important now, such as emotions and today's experiences and less on thinking about the future. While it is obvious that there is some physical decline as people age – from the age of 20 onwards short-term memory is impaired and it is less easy to focus attention – nevertheless, it appears that older people can learn strategies for improving general memory, as well as can younger people. Motivation seems to be the key.

'The human brain does not operate like a computer. It does not process all information evenly. Rather, motivation directs our attention to goal-relevant information and away from irrelevant information. We see what matters to us.' 6

Walking with my cousin through a city street new to both of us, at the end of the day, because I am interested in buildings I am likely to have made a note of the approximate dates for the building of the various properties, whether they were 19th century or before or whether they were modern. I can guarantee that for my cousin, he will have noted the names of all the pubs!

In tests for what is now regarded as Emotional Intelligence, necessary for understanding and interacting with other people, it is older people who score highly. Although the ability to acquire new knowledge would appear to decline, emotional intelligence is at its highest in old age, enabling old people better to cope with what appears to younger people to be the unbearable stresses of old age. It would appear that their interest is in people, rather than in the processing of factual information, such as particle physics or electronics, for which a good IQ is an advantage. Our understanding of intelligence has, in the past, been geared to what is of interest to young people, rather than the older generation.

Emotional intelligence was recognised as recently as the 1960s (the first useful IQ test, the Binet-Simon test came out in 1905), when it was recognised that older people had a better understanding of emotional states and of ways of dealing with them than those who are younger. While they share with adolescents' strong emotional feelings, they understand them in a way that softens the impact. It is believed that the uncontrolled behaviour of youngsters up to their early 20s can be explained by the development of the brain. It appears that the synapses in the frontal cortex, the forefront of the brain and the seat of the emotions, are the last to be joined up, so that behaviour at that time is illogical. It is the age of the angry young man, full of ideals and the belief that he can change the world. The older man is no less angry but he has become the grumpy old man, who knows people for what they are and that there are limits as to how things can be changed; but he also knows we occasionally need to shout about them. In societies where the wisdom of old age is still respected, younger people will listen to these outbursts from the older generation and learn from them. In our society these grumpy old men are just seen as cantankerous, they become the butt of jokes. It is yet another way in which society can add to the feeling of isolation among the elderly.

If emotional intelligence is not recognised as a valuable asset, society can justify marginalising those who could be using it for the benefit of society as a whole.

Some studies done among the Ju/'hoansi (pronounced juntwasi) of Botswana in the 1980s[7] reveal surprising views on and interpretations of the behaviour of old people. For the J/'hoansi, the desire to live alone was classed as a form of mental illness. 'Only a crazy person would live alone', said one.

There is never any suggestion that one should live alone in order not to burden the younger generation. On the contrary, everyone was taught from being a child of the duty to repay the care they have received by looking after the older generation. Only someone with a 'crippled heart' would refuse to do that. Not only is the older person not expected to express gratitude, but it is taken for granted they will be cantankerous and constantly complaining about the care they get. Failing to do so would be interpreted as a sign of failing intellect because in J/'hoansi society, complaining and grumbling is a cultural game played at all ages. It is play-acting and never taken too seriously.

A Story from Botswana

Gumi, a frail 83-year-old was sleeping in her hut, next to a fire, Despite the fact that the mid-afternoon sun was unbearably hot outside, her daughter led a European visitor into the hut and roughly wakened Gumi, who quickly became alert and entered into the conversation with interest and vigour. The conversation was not easy, as she was very deaf, and her daughter cupped her hand close to Gumi's ear as she spoke to her. It was not long before Gumi produced a tirade of questions. What have you brought for me? I want some medicine. Have you brought some clothes for me? Give me some beads. I want 'hxaro' (gifts).

At length, her daughter interrupted her with laughter in her voice, "Oh stop asking for 'hxaro.' Stop going on about it." But Gumi was undeterred.

Later, when the researcher mentioned the incident to some elders of the tribe, they understood perfectly what had been going on when 'hxaro' was mentioned. Wonderful! "Even as old as she is, she still knows how to talk nicely. Her thoughts are still sound."

In J/'hoansi society, her language was considered appropriate for the situation of gift exchange. She clearly knew the protocol; she knew her entitlement; her ability to make demands showed she was still of sound mind and sound understanding. 8

So, in a similar way, the word 'grumble' in the English language has no sinister context for the listener. It is an insignificant grouse, a minor annoyance, almost a subject for humour. The grumbling of old people is not likely to be taken too seriously. Yet, the grumbles are often symptoms of that deeper malaise, the frustrations of old people that their voice is no longer heard, their ideas are no longer of any significance. They don't matter. Sitting on train zooming its way from the Lake District to Devon, the usual indecipherable message came over the loudspeaker a few miles outside of Wolverhampton. As I was expecting to go all the way to Devon, I did not bother to ask anyone what it was all about. The train stopped and people got off. Engrossed as I was in reading a newspaper, it took a while before I realised we were reversing out of the station. What was even more worrying, it appeared there was no one else in the carriage. It was even longer before my worst fears were confirmed and the train attendant came along and crossly asked what I was doing there. "Didn't you hear my announcement?"

"No! Sorry!"

I began to feel like a naughty child who had not listened to the teacher.

"Oh well! We are going back to Crewe. You will just have to find another train there," and off she trotted.

I felt very deserted and lonely, not because I was not capable of finding another train, but because my hearing was not up to interpreting loudspeaker announcements. I felt isolated mentally and was indeed physically isolated from the lack of any other passenger on the train.

It is not that the older generation do not understand modern technology. It is not always geared to their needs or they sometimes just do not need it. 'You haven't got a mobile?' they ask incredulously. It is not that we are not perfectly capable of learning how to use mobile phones, but why should we feel outcasts because quite simply we may not need one. I have had a couple in the past but in both cases the battery ran down, and it appears that that means you need to buy a new phone. As I have no one at home to phone, it means I very seldom need to use it. For an emergency, it is of course ideal, but fortunately emergencies are rare. To maintain a mobile, I would have to have it on charge regularly, remember to put it in my bag every time I go out and then a year or more might go by before I ever needed to use it. I just do not think I need a mobile, as do those who wander down the street apparently talking to themselves. At the tops of their voices they shout, 'Did you see her hairdo last night!' Is it so urgent to find out if a friend saw someone the evening before and if they noticed a new hairdo? How urgent is it to have an answer to that question? I begin to suspect these phone addicts are suffering from withdrawal symptoms through lack of contact with another human being (apart from those anonymous people cluttering up the street). Could it be that these people are really the lonely ones?

One elderly friend said to me, "I am never bored."

That did not surprise me; she does wonderful embroidery, bakes on a daily basis and always has her knitting bag on a stool by her chair.

"No, I am not ever bored!" she says. "If I am waiting for a bus and there is nothing else to do, I watch the aeroplanes flying over and wonder about their passengers."

For her, if she wants to telephone a friend, she can easily wait until she gets home.

In western society, there is a real problem of loneliness for elderly people who have all their lives been marginalised through lack of money, lack of education, of role models or of aspiration – life's failures – and as these people get older, their situation becomes more desolate. This is a symptom of society's failure and failure of political will. Only political measures, coming from an understanding that these people from birth are victims rather than failures, can provide support for them, not as an afterthought in their old age but from their very earliest years.

For the middle classes, for the most part, loneliness in old age should not a big problem. Living alone for some people can be quite satisfactory, if not entirely desirable, and there are many clubs, societies, bingo halls, not to mention pubs and churches offering company. A feeling of loneliness for this group of people is more likely to come from perceived, if not real, neglect by their own relatives and sometimes friends, who become so important to them as they grow older.

It is not so much individual loneliness that is the real problem but society's isolation of the older generation, old people who have so much to offer but whose voice is seldom listened to. Ageism has been endemic in western society since the time of the Greeks. It is not new. The word 'old' is itself, for the most part, a word denoting something that is no longer useful, past its sell-by date, antique, slightly despicable: old fashioned, old hat, old lag, old maid. The fact that this century will see the percentage of elderly people compared to the rest of society rise and rise is not likely to heal the rift between young and old, not least because of the greater cost of looking after those less able to look after themselves and who may need expensive medical care.

This is already becoming more than just a talking point, and in some countries, it appears cigarette smoking may be an unexpected way of dealing with it. In 1997, the BBC reported what they called the Philip Morris approach to the problem (the Morris firm have been making cigarettes since 1847), when the company noted that *early deaths in the Czech Republic caused by smoking reduced health and housing costs for the elderly and so have saved them £147 million*! 10

I did not ever expect to see headlines in a newspaper such as, *Pensioner crime wave marks the rise of the 'Saga lout'* 9, which goes on to say that statistics supplied by police forces show a rise of between 15% and 25% in the numbers of pensioners being arrested. It goes on to quote Bill Tupman a criminologist at Exeter University, who believes there is now a far harsher attitude towards the elderly.

He says, 'Police and courts are now less likely to take pity on poor granddad in the dock.'

This 'grey crime' and the attention now being focussed on crime by the elderly is being recorded also in France, Japan and Israel. It is a worldwide problem.

What is now quite clear is that the 21st century is facing a demographic change that is completely new. For the first time ever, in the western world or elsewhere, there will be a large proportion of the population that are elderly, and it will need new thinking, a new plan. People aged 65 and over will outnumber children under 5. A quarter of all children born today can expect to live to be 100. The only place I can think of where there is any precedent is in Okinawa, the islands to the south of the main islands of Japan. There no one would comment on the fact that a 100-year-old woman decided to give up farming for running a market stall. Old age is a continuation of life. They would not understand the mindset of westerners, who feel they have worked all their lives for others and for their families and that when you retire from work, you decide to centre life on yourself, because you deserve it! They know all too well that being useful in society, doing paid or unpaid work, is what keeps them an integral part of that society. That is what they go on living for. Loneliness never becomes a problem.

One major role that the older generation play in so-called primitive societies is that of governing or providing advice to the younger generation. 'Elders' still exist in many native American Indian tribes, such as the Mohegan tribe of Connecticut. The tribal elders, consisting of four men and three women, oversee all cultural matters, religion and justice. The tribal elders of the Chumash Indians must be at least 50 years old and its governing board of seven members is responsible for, among other things, creating a strong bond with youth. In Africa, it is to the tribal elders that Wangari Mathi, a Nobel Prize winner, appealed in order to calm down the youths of the Kikuyu, the Luos, Luhyas and Kalenjins, who were indulging in a wave of violence during a presidential election campaign in 2008. The elders there have influence with the young. In politics in the western world, especially in the UK, the political leaders are no longer elder statesmen – they get younger and younger. Apart from the retention of an elderly political icon, how easy will this be to reverse?

If in the 21st century, western society has neither the desire nor the economic resources to look after the elderly and they see no role for the elderly as a source of wisdom, of inspiration or of spiritual knowledge, then perhaps the only role left in our aging society is for the young old to look after the really old. Improved healthcare has ensured that people stay healthier for longer and looking at organisations such as Age UK, their workers and staff seem to be mostly already retired. Perhaps that is the inevitable trend.

I took a friend of mine to a meeting today. She is nearly 80 and lives alone on an isolated hill farm at about 600 feet. Her house is a neat, converted barn and flowers at her front door give you a smiling welcome. She has no children, and her nearest relatives are 100 miles away. Her husband died some years ago, and in recent years, she has had several eyesight operations. Arthritis is making walking difficult.

When I rang to offer her a lift, she said, "I would like to come but I am not sure I have time."

She decided to come anyway. I said that I was surprised that she was so busy.

"Oh yes," she said, "I do seem to get involved."

I knew she did the minutes for the Parish Meeting and several other organisations, that she was in the church choir and went to painting classes.

"I would like to do less but no one else seems to want to take these jobs on." But then, she added, without prompting, "But, you know, I am never lonely."

Chapter 9 Notes

1. Cynthia Moss, Elephant Memories (p 73) 2000 Univ Chicago Press
2. Dept Health statistics 2010

3. Michael K. Kusmano, The Cultural Context of Aging (p395) Ed. Jay Sokolovsky 2009 Praeger
4. Orsolya Lelkes EC Policy analyst at the European Centre for Social Welfare, Policy and Research 2008 www.euro.centre.org/lelkes
5. Arthur Tone PNS Paper, 2010 (?) "A snapshot of the age distribution of psychological well-being in the United States" (Source Economist 27/12/10
6. Laura Carstensen, Director of the Stanford Center on Longevity, Stanford University Policies and Politics for an Aging America Growing Old or Living Longer Take Your Choice Lecture 2006 National Academy of Sciences
7. Harriet. G. Rosenberg, The Cultural Context of Aging, ibid
8. Ibid
9. Tracy McVeigh Observer 21.11.10
10. South Lakeland Magazine Nov 2011 Dick Brown – Trustee Age Concern South Lakeland

* Closer Magazine 19 February 2010

So, if a people deserted by their family, living for many years alone and without any real friends, do not necessarily consider themselves lonely, what is loneliness? We all know that in a dysfunctional family the feeling of loneliness can be far greater than for someone with no living family.

Chapter 10
Senility

Poem from 'Now We are Sixty' by Christopher Matthew, a tribute to A A Milne's 'Now we are Six'

MOTHER

(after DISOBEDIENCE)

Tom, Clare, Crispin and Clementine,
Oliver, Jane and me
Gave much thought to old Mother When she was ninety-three.
Tom, Clare, Crispin and Clementine
Oliver, Jane and their three
Did plenty of talking and fussing and squawking, but left all the doing to me.
One day
Our dear old Mother, Dressed in her Sunday best, Left a note in the kitchen:
"I don't want to be a pest.
I've just popped out to New Zealand,
I've gone on a bit of a spree,
I'll visit my brother, his wife and my mother, and be back in time for tea."
The police Alerted all mobiles:
"Elderly woman in grey

Answers to Mrs MacDougall, Could be heading your way.
Thinks she's
Off to New Zealand, Handle with extra care.
She could be doolally, so be nice and jolly – and try not to
give her a scare."
Tom, Clare,
Crispin and Clementine (Known to her friends as Clem), Got
straight
Onto the blower, and she said that one
couldn't blame them.
Clementine Said, "Well I never!"
"Frankly," she said, "if she
Can't be left on her own, she should be in a home
Somewhere nice down in Kent by the sea."
Poor dear silly old Mother
Was found feeding ducks in the park, With a tramp
With a trolley from Tesco Piled like a nomadic camp.
She said, "Lovely to see you –
This is my young brother, Roy,
He's such a nice chap, and he's not changed a scrap since
he was a dear little boy."
(To be spoken, very solemnly and clearly – as though to a
backward child) "TC
CC
OJ and me Can't look
After you M*****, Now you are ninety-three"
"Stuff and Nonsense," said M*****. "If I can cross the sea,
And visit my brother, his wife and my mother, there's
nothing much wrong with ME!"
Is senility something we can joke about? Why not?

Senility as a term is now apparently old hat. In these days of medical research, it has to be Alzheimer's or dementia or Lewy bodies or one of many others. Alzheimer's was named after Alois Alzheimer, a German doctor in Frankfurt, who took an interest in a 51-year-old patient called Auguste Deter, who showed odd behaviour and had a loss of short-term memory. Little did she know it, but five years later in 1906, after she died, an examination of her brain, together with the notes Alzheimer had made of the progress of her disease, enabled him to associate her symptoms with 'amyloid plaques and neurofibrillary tangles' in her brain: Alzheimer's disease.

So, it came about that in the west, symptoms of old age which had always been known previously as 'senility' and were accepted as natural deterioration became a medical condition. The symptoms of senility include changes in behaviour, in speech and in memory; in moodiness; and in the ability to dress, feed or to look after oneself. As medical conditions, these ageing symptoms acquired a whole raft of names. Give something a name and something new comes into existence. Sometimes, like the word 'cancer', it may be something new and frightening.

Senility has a much gentler sound, and it comes from the Latin word simply meaning 'old.' The word expresses the changes that most people expect to come about with age, but these changes are viewed very differently in other cultures. They are often seen as a stage of life, rather than an illness. In tribal societies, people are likely to be much more matter of fact, 'What can you expect when people get old? Of course, they change. The skin wrinkles, the arms are less strong, the legs do not move so fast, the sight dims, the hearing deteriorates.'

We now have palliatives for all these changes, but we are beginning to understand that it is changes in the brain, that is the ageing of the brain, that produces senile behaviour. Up to now, most of these changes have been shown to be as irreversible as wrinkling of the skin. So, we might even find that it is helpful to accept that, as it is accepted in many societies, old age inevitably brings about physical and mental changes. Such an attitude creates fewer frustrations, especially when it becomes clear that medical science does not yet know the answers to many of the problems of old age.

In 1988, at an anthropological conference in Zagreb[2], an Indian anthropologist gave a paper on the long lives of elders in the hills of northern India. A questioner asked about the prevalence of dementia in India, but the speaker did not appear to understand. To clarify, the questioner used the words, 'senile dementia, Alzheimer's disease.'

Despite the speaker's knowledge of Indian gerontology, he still did not understand. Other Americans in the audience tried to explain – a blank. Then someone shouted out, 'Crazy old people!'

That caused consternation, but there was still no meeting of minds. In India, old people are not crazy, they are just old people. In contrast, in western culture, old people have diseases which require medical intervention with results that may be far from satisfactory. It may even make the end of life a long, drawn-out and miserable experience.

It does not have to be like that. Among the Palaungs of Northern Burma (Myanmar), old people are said to live happy lives. Their old age is attributed to virtue achieved in a previous life and they are so venerated that to step on their shadow is a bad omen. As a result, they are looked after, their needs are satisfied and their value to the community is respected. Even young girls, soon after marriage, like to appear older than they are in order to gain that respect. On another continent, the elders in Native American tribes are often accredited with special powers or with magic, such as in the case of a Hopi Indian, who claimed to have the ability to bring to life the skins of the dogs which hung on the walls of his house and to command them to dance. Other Hopi old men were able to turn themselves into birds to escape an oncoming tide of water. From our civilised point of view, these people were clearly suffering from hallucinations, perhaps dementia, but their own communities accepted their behaviour, sometimes honouring them for it, sometimes simply tolerating it.

Not that all tribal societies tolerate the very old who were physically weak and senile. Ritual suicide was common, as was assisted suicide in communities as far apart as the Eskimos in the Arctic to the Ju/'hoansi of Botswana. These are usually communities where famine is a frequent threat. Nevertheless, as Dr Leo Simonds states[3], 'The experience of ageing in primitive societies seems to be more smoothly tapered and the onset of senescence less abrupt and freer of traumatic transitional phases than in modern civilisation. No haunting calendar, no chronological deadline makes each birthday a well-marked milestone on the road to death. This keen awareness of chronological age is a modern experience of ageing which has little place in primitive life.'

He goes on to say, "…primitive cultures are frequently so well adapted to the capacities of old people that old age can become a more enviable period than the youthful years."

In India, what appears to be the almost instinctive desire the world over for the middle aged to care for their elderly parents is reinforced by their underlying Hindu philosophy of veneration towards their elders. The reciprocal indebtedness of children towards their parents is deeply ingrained and easily practised because of their intergenerational style of living. A Bengali man was washing some sheets in a pond near their family house. The sheets were from the bed of his frail mother who was incontinent. He was surprised to be asked about this.

He said, "Caring for parents is the child's duty... For example, when I am old and have a bowel movement, my son will clean it up and won't ask, 'Why did you do it there?' This is what she did for us when we was young. When I am old and dying, who will take me to go to pee and defecate? My children will have to do it."

4 Indian daughters-in-law, related only by marriage to their parents-in-law care in the same way for them because they look upon it as a deeply social-moral duty. They may sometimes view it as a tedious burden but there is a spiritual reward and to do otherwise is unthinkable.

While certainly to the Indian mind it seems obvious that children have a duty towards their ageing parents, under the influence of western philosophy, science and morality, we often view it every differently. A child is born because its parents desire it, and the perpetuation of the species requires it. It is the duty of the parents and it is obviously good sense that the parents should nurture and care for the child, not in any way because the parents have any expectation of return for their care. A child does not ask to be born and their duty is towards the future generation, rather than towards care for their parents in their old age.

Their children must take priority. This would seem to be a justification for parents to concentrate their resources on their own children. Hive off the folks to a psychiatric unit, an old people's home, a residential care home or a Sun City retirement community – your choice depending on your social stratum or your purse!

While this argument can seem to offer a logical justification for residential and care homes, especially if the family is separated by distance, many people even in the west do feel an emotional obligation to their elderly parents, especially if they have retained a loving relationship with them throughout their lives.

The Japanese have a slightly different view of where responsibility lies for the welfare of the older generation. It has always been seen as a duty of eldest sons to care for their parents in old age and this is a duty enshrined in Confucian philosophy and politically enforced from the reign of the Meiji emperors onwards. Nevertheless, the elderly have a reciprocal duty. Filial piety towards elderly parents is balanced by an acceptance of dependency on the part of the elders and also by their sense that it is their moral duty not to become a burden. The elderly must bear some of the responsibility themselves to the extent that some blame will attach to them if they have not looked after their own physical and mental health.[5] There is seen to be a limit to the burden of care that the elderly had a right to impose on their children. To undertake physical and mental exercise and to remain fit as long as possible was not only something that was obviously desirable, but a duty.

This is of some concern to many elderly people and so they frequent the numerous pokkuri, the 'swift death' temples, where they buy amulets to protect them from the diseases of old age and pray for a peaceful, and most importantly, for a timely death. The rate of suicide among Japanese aged 65 and over is higher than anywhere in the western world. In 2003, it was 35.3 per 100,000 persons; by comparison, in the USA, the figures for that year were 27.4 for men and only 4.43 for women.[6]

In all the developed world, Japan has been the first country to feel the impact of an ageing population. In 2005, over 20% were over 65 years old and 25% of the over 65s were aged over 80! By 2050, it is estimated that 40% of the population will be over 65.[7] Since the 1970s, political steps have been undertaken to forestall the effects of this, but they have been overtaken by events. For instance, they designated seats at the front of buses as 'silver seats', reserved for the elderly and disabled, but most of the people on the buses are now old people anyway! Although dependency of the old upon their children is still encouraged, it is the movement of young people to the towns away from their parents' homes that has started to break up the pattern of intergenerational living, and new solutions for the care of the elderly have had to be found. One much-favoured solution is the building of a separate space for the elderly in the younger generation's property, the elders living close enough so that, 'the soup won't get cold', when it is brought to them by the daughter or daughter-in-law. This, however, is only possible for the wealthy and the number of intergenerational households is down from 55% in 1985 to 45% in 2005.[8] – although still high by the standards of Western Europe and the USA.

What follows relies heavily on research done by Brenda R Jenike and John W Traphagan[9], living and working in Japan. When, in 1990, the Japanese government began to realise that a forward-looking plan was needed, they produced the Gold Plan. This was state funded. People were encouraged to be as independent as possible, so the state paid for day care homes and an army of day care assistants. When they ran out of day care nurses, they imported them from the Philippines. The state also paid for long-term residential care. Within five years, the cost was escalating to such an extent that the plan was modified, tightening up the qualifications needed for access to care. By the year 2000, it was clear that the costs had become completely out of hand, so to cope with it, a new scheme was introduced, which required a compulsory pension contribution from everyone over the age of 40. The pension was expected to cover 50% of the national care costs for those over 65, while the remainder was shared between national and local government and the recipients of the care.

This new system was greatly welcomed because the elderly were able to choose the kind of care they wanted. It also led to a proliferation of new institutions. For instance, the number of homes for those with Alzheimer's went up from 369 in 2000 to over 4000 in 2005. It also doubled the cost of care between those two dates, mainly because of the increase in the number of people needing it. Commercialisation and the Japanese passion for gadgets started to take over. Do you want a rehabilitation manual or a book of recreational games for the elderly? There is a big selection at the bookshop. Would you like a robotic grandchild to keep you company? Your LTCI (Long Term Care Insurance) may possibly fund it. Are you finding it difficult to feed yourself? The spoon-feeding robot arm, operated by the chin, might be cheaper than a day care visitor. Then there is the wheelchair that responds to voice commands. The emphasis is all on looking after your own needs as long as possible. It chimes with the Japanese cultural imperative not to overburden your children with your care. The move is towards a view of the elderly as entitled consumers and as far as possible to offer them independence away from institutions,

Also what appears to be happening in Western Europe and North America, where elderly people, while they are able, often prefer to go on living in their own homes, and unexpectedly perhaps, most people over the age of 90 in the western world still continue to live on their own. The big problem arises when they cannot deal with all their daily needs, but from the point of view of psychological well-being, to remain in their familiar surroundings is the preferred option. When this becomes impractical, a dilemma arises for relatives or for those who themselves come face to face with the fact that their lives are on a downward slope and they realise they may not be able to cope on their own.

Surprisingly, the moment of discovery from their doctor that their future is about to change is for many people less fearful than one might imagine. A blogger called 'Don', a doctor who lives in San Diego, describes his feelings vividly.

'The quiet after the storm: it's raining in San Diego – finally.

'It's quiet now, water trickles down the spout and drops are still splattering from the eves. It's soothing. I slept well, better than any night the past week. A warm glow, an inner peace fills me. I'm content and happy.

'It's a strange aftereffect of the news I received yesterday. I don't yet fully understand it, but after the first shock of the news that I had Alzheimer's and a moment of sadness and fear, this sudden wave of peace and serenity.'

The early signs that something was wrong with him were subtle, according to the 73-year-old, 'I was getting angry a lot. I would fly off the handle at the grandkids.' He also got lost driving down familiar streets.

His first thoughts after being diagnosed were of some of his shut-in patients 'lying there like vegetables.' But the darkness didn't last, "You can either just roll over and let it come or begin living your life because you're not dead," he told me in the living room of his Lake San Marcos condo.

Ironically, there are pluses to Alzheimer's, according to Don. He said he's become more focused on what's important to him, "I stay in contact with everybody I love."

He wrote in his blog, 'It's strange, but being diagnosed with Alzheimer's has made a profound difference in me – for the better!'

'I'm gonna die? So what!'

He confided, 'When I was younger, I was always waiting for or reaching for another goal, instead of living in the moment.'

'I'm comfortable with where I'm at. I'm not preoccupied with something you can't control.'10

Glen Campbell[11], the world-renowned country music singer (selling 45 million records in his career to date) was diagnosed with Alzheimer's in 2011 and his reaction was to undertake a final world tour. He knew he might forget his lines, so he had an autocue, or he made a joke of it with his audience. The audience responded as they always did, not to his jokes but to the skill he still showed in his playing and the passion he put into his singing.

That was so much part of who he was that it never failed him, and he never failed to inspire.

His wife says, "The power music has to preserve what Campbell has left is on display any time he picks up a guitar. His fingers appear to have forgotten nothing and still float over the strings."

The lyrics of one of his latest songs runs, *This is not the road I wanted for us/but now that it's here/I want to make one thing perfectly clear/all I want to be for you is strong. /Some days I'm so confused, Lord/my past gets in my way/I need the ones I love more/more and more each day*. It's powerful and heart-breaking music.

This seems to suggest the idea that maybe senility is far more a problem for friends and relatives than it is for the sufferer yet even for relatives it can bring – unbelievably – great joy.

There is a remarkable photo diary produced by an American, Philip Toledano,12 about the last three years of his father's life. It started when his mother died. His father was then 96 and Philip discovered that he was losing his memory, a fact that his mother had hidden from the family. At first, Philip's frequent visits to see his father are deeply distressing – his father's insistence on eating eggs and only eggs, his habit of feeding his dinner surreptitiously to his dog, the notes he leaves around the house ('Where is everyone?', 'What's going on?'), his apparent sexual desire for Philip's wife, Carla, ('What an amazing figure!'). His father spends a great deal of time on the toilet. After finishing the job, he would start to put on his trousers and then say, 'Wait a second – I have to go.' Gently reasoning with him, the only response is a withering look, the look of a father who cannot believe he has such a stupid child.

Philip's father cannot come to terms with the death of his wife, a woman he loved dearly, so Philip plays a game with him. Although he was taken to the funeral, he has no memory of it, but he is prepared to accept the story that his wife has gone to Paris. They make up stories about what she is doing there. She has gone to run a famous circus. Then the circus is acted out. Philip puts his head in the lion's mouth, swings on the trapeze, treads the high wire. It is all such fun! His father loves telling stories, and jokes! He recalls the Italian fishmonger telling him as a ten-year-old, 'Don't squeeze the fish, its eyes will bulge.'

His dad loves to talk about the past, his days as a minor film star, his successful business career, his love of painting. He can still admire a sunset and be fascinated by the expression on the face of his dog. There are occasional moments of lucidity, 'Where's Mum?' He tells him that she has just gone out to the shop. Everything is normal once again.

Philip can never quite relinquish thoughts of days past, the days when his mother and father were young, ambitious and capable, but he begins to learn to enjoy his time with the father he now has, to treasure every moment he can spend with him, 'to know that we loved each other nakedly, without embarrassment.'

I think Philip would have understood the Buddhist teaching about time and about change, 'Do not encumber your mind with useless thoughts. What good does it do to brood on the past or anticipate the future? Remain in the simplicity of the present moment.'13 And again, 'Somehow, in the process of denying that things are always changing, we lose our sense of the sacredness of life.'14

Philip learnt to rejoice even in those moments of frustration with his father. In an extraordinary way, his father was able to give Philip something more precious than he could ever have imagined.

To understand what Buddhists mean by living in the present is one thing. To allow that idea to motivate the way you live is quite another. Buddhist philosophers also know how hard this is to achieve and they spend a lifetime pursuing it. It goes against the optimistic nature we are born with – the optimism about the future that we need in order to survive. This optimism is strengthened in western culture with the expectations which we are encouraged to adopt, the ambitions we have, the constant looking towards the future and the search for perfect happiness that motivates our thoughts and actions. These attitudes create a great barrier to accepting the present. We live in hope, the hope that there will one day be a cure for all illnesses and solutions for the problems of ageing; when we discover we are chasing rainbows, depression takes over. From the day we are born, we all live with a death sentence, but we do not want to think about it. When, however, the movement towards it suddenly becomes obvious, perhaps in a doctor's surgery, there is still no reason why we cannot go on living in the way that gives us and those around us the most satisfying reward. Those who achieve this, and many do, surprise us with their amazing acceptance of the inevitable.

Louis Theroux, that seeker out of bizarre experiences, visited the Banner Alzheimer's Institute in Phoenix, Arizona. His televised report included a sequence filmed between a middle-aged man and his mother, who was in a late stage of dementia. The lady's vocabulary had been reduced to one word, repeated over and over again, 'Golly, golly, golly golly golly', and then, 'golly, golly, golly; golly, golly, golly', at a higher pitch.

He was the only one of her relatives to visit because everyone else had become so distressed at seeing this woman mumbling 'Golly, golly', as she unsteadily negotiated obstacles, unseen by anyone else. Then without warning, she came towards her son and looked up at him very, very intently. There was a moment of recognition and she flung her arms around him, clinging tightly and uncontrollably. He responded to the embrace and they just stood there. I guess he had never given any woman such an embrace, much less his own mother. In that moment, the mother was showing a love hidden inside her, the love of a mother for a baby; the pride of a mother in a growing boy; the adoration of a mother for a capable adult; the love that because of her culture she was too embarrassed ever to have expressed once he was no longer a baby. He said afterwards that the moment was more precious to him than anything else, and it would never be forgotten.

Even in people in the late stages of dementia, there are flashes that reveal and reaffirm a person's identity. The wonderful thing is that they are no longer self-conscious about their feelings, inhibitions are removed, and they do not need to consider how people will react to them. As social beings, this may seem unacceptable to us; tragic and no longer human. To the sufferer, it might come as a great release.

In the UK, bizarrely, as a result of political decisions, Alzheimer's may often be conveniently considered a social rather than a medical problem, so that the free care offered to the sick is not available to Alzheimer's sufferers. It is on the other hand, according to the medical community, a medical condition. Nevertheless, seeing some of the extreme symptoms of dementia as horrifying symptoms of a disease, rather than as a natural process, may actually lead to an exacerbation of their condition. Medical provisions are in the main palliatives and may actually cause a worsening of behaviour. In addition, the way elderly people are treated often results in stress, such as when they are spoken to like children or simply seen as 'cases' that have to be brought under control. The need for respect for our identity as a mature person remains in us long after other mental faculties have declined.

Mental disorientation often occurs when vulnerable people are moved from one environment to another, and vital misunderstandings arise. One patient (why do we still call them 'patients'?) called Margaret screamed uncontrollably when she had a bath. It turned out that she was not being awkward but suffered when water got into her ears. A waterproof bonnet might have solved the problem but putting it on did not fit in with the nurse's schedule. This lady had 29 changes in her medication, which apparently led to her becoming more confused and more aggressive and it was only when she was returned to her original medication that there was any sign of improvement.

When she declared, "I don't like this place; it's the whole thing I don't like," the nurses put it down to her dementia but it was simply an expression of genuine unhappiness. 16 Such examples of disastrous changes in medication can be found over and over again.

In another example of misunderstanding, there was a woman who was a very difficult patient. She became incontinent, she had to be restrained in a wheelchair, she refused hygienic care and she started to disrobe in public. In desperation, they moved her to another unit, where the staff had quite a different ethos. The nurse who was given the task of looking after her realised that this behaviour was in part the result of anger at having to be dependent on others when she had always been proudly independent. In addition, the lady had a great fear about her own condition and what the future held for her.

Understanding this need for independence, she was allowed to structure her day however she wanted. The nurses also showed that they were not appalled by her behaviour, but they offered her respect and support. As a result, she showed such a remarkable improvement that her previous staff hardly recognised her.[17]

The simple change that enabled this improvement to occur seemed to be because she was being treated not so much as a patient that needed control and medication but as a normal person with abnormal worries and what she needed most of all was emotional support. While not denying that there may be physical changes in the brain of an old person for which our medical knowledge can provide certain palliatives, what is normal and acceptable and what is abnormal in the old is culturally determined.

Experimental work in the USA by people such as William Thomas[15], who founded the 'Greenhouse Project', emphasises the need to treat the person and not the patient. The 'Greenhouses' offer homes rather than a custodial environment; they consider the needs of the resident and not the timetable of the staff; they try to design a small community which is also in touch with outside world. So, his experimental units are in ordinary houses sited within a community. They are small, with only seven or eight people, each of whom has their own separate living area. The residents work together as a family, helping with the daily chores and preparing the meals, insofar as they were able. The people who look after them are not nurses but take on the roles of carers, companions and housekeepers. This is a developing project, but one that suggests new ways of housing people who are unable any longer to live on their own.

So what can we say about senility? Medical science has identified, analysed and offered cures for many of the physical disability of old age and as a result we live longer healthier lives. But medical science is still and will continue to be an experimental and an inexact science and inevitably concentrates on the physical rather than the emotional problems of old age. Perhaps above all, doctors have to learn a most difficult thing when for them the purpose of their work is to cure illness; that is they have to know when they must accept that their work has come to an end; and society must be able to be confident in their judgement.

Psychology is a science that explains behaviour, but it is also an art – an art that compassionate people can often acquire without formal training. We know that but too often the demands of institutional organisation and lack of finance result in the denial of the respect that even the most senile deserve.

From comparative studies of other cultures, we learn the value of acceptance, something we have lost because our sciences have given us such high hopes and expectations.

People grow old, why should that fact frighten the young? Old people in general, despite their infirmities, are more content with their lives than younger generations, and they can laugh at themselves!

'What have I got to remember today?' 'Remember to keep breathing!'

In those societies where the elderly are venerated, the young are not frightened to grow old. Perhaps this is a lesson well worth learning!

Our problem is our attitude to change. It is easy to accept and look forward to the physical changes that occur as a baby becomes a child and a child becomes an adolescent. The particular beauty of youth for others of the same species has a purpose – procreation. Our society is one focussed on the young but in some societies, they see a different kind of beauty in old age because old age also has a purpose. If it were not so, once a human child is born and reared, the death of the parent would follow quickly after. Why do we go on living so long after bearing and rearing children? It is far from universal in the animal kingdom. A male octopus dies soon after mating. A female octopus may stay alive for several months after laying the eggs, protecting them from predators and gently blowing oxygenated water over them to keep them alive. During this time, she eats nothing and as soon as the eggs are ready to hatch, she dies. The human species is not like that. There is a genuine Darwinian logic about the fact that we may live many years following procreation and caring for the young. It is that older people have the time, the experience and the love to nurture the future generation. The love grandparents have for their children and of children for their grandparents is in the genes. Our lives are like a daffodil, the flower, so beautiful in its prime, its beauty designed to attract insects to fertilise the seed. When it fades, the leaves remain, but in their way, they are just as beautiful. Though they are no longer a vibrant yellow, they are a shiny green and still very much alive. Their purpose is to provide nourishment for the developing bulb.

When we consider senility, Andrew Motion puts it very succinctly: 'I am here…I matter!'

Chapter 10 Notes

1. Christopher Matthew: Now we are 60, 1999: John Murray, London
2. Conference in Zagreb on Old Age, 1988
3. Simonds, Leo. The Journal of Gerontology vol 1 Issue 1 Part 1 Pp 72-951946
4. The Cultural Context of Aging ed. Jay Sokolovsky: 2009; Praeger. Westport USA; Sarah Lamb: Elder Residences and Outsourced Sons. p 419
5. Ibid Transforming the Cultural Scripts for Aging and Elder Care in Japan: Chap 17; Brenda R.Jenike and John W. Traphagan p247
6. Japanese statistical yearbook 2007
7. Japan statistical yearbook 2008
8. The Cultural Context of Aging ed. Jay Sokolovsky: 2009; Praeger. Westport USA; Transforming the Cultural Scripts for Aging and Elder Care in Japan: Chap 17; Brenda R.Jenike and John W. Traphagan
9. The BLOG of Don from San Diego California called 'The Trip Over'

10. Glen Campbell
11. Toledano, Philip; 2010; Days with my Father; PQ Blackwell in association with Chronicle Books LLC
12. Oliver and Danielle Föllini; Buddhist Offerings: Dilgo Khyentse Rimpoche, page 18, April Stewart, Tabori and Chang, New York Thames and Hudson, London (no date)
13. Ibid Pema Chödrön, 30 April
14. Thomas, William; 1996 Life Worth Living; VanderWyke and Burnham
15. The Cultural Context of Aging; ed. Jay Sokolovsky: 2009; Praeger. Westport USA; Chap. 44 Beyond the Institution: Athena McLean
16. Ibid

Chapter 11
The Death Problem

Cowards die many times before their deaths;
The valiant never taste death but once.
Of all the wonders that I yet have heard,
It seems to me most strange that men should fear,
Seeing that death, a necessary end,
Will come when it will come.

Shakespeare – Julius Caesar

Why do we have to die? Perhaps our most basic instinct is to stay alive. Survival is one of the most important drivers of our actions. The search for the elixir of life, a potion that would ensure immortality was a major concern of the ancient Chinese emperors, of the Indians, of the Persians and others. In medieval times, the alchemists spent their lives trying to identify a substance that would offer eternal youth. Today, the search continues with crinology offering the hope that by freezing the body immediately after death in liquid nitrogen at a temperature of 196 degrees centigrade, at some time in the future we will be able not only bring that person back to life but overcome all the damage that the freezing process inflicts, as well as the disease that caused the death.

You can see all the gory details of this process if you go to *(http://topdocumentaryfilms.com/cryonics-death-deep-freeze/)* and one can understand that if you happen to have $80,000 to spare ($40,000 if you just want your head preserved in liquid nitrogen), you have nothing to lose, but the truth is that they are only just beginning to learn how to preserve a single organ in ice, such as a kidney for transplant, and at present, the idea has no credibility at all. It raises the question too of what it would mean for the world if we could all be guaranteed immortality. How many people could the world hold? Do we really want to live in a world where Caligula, Ivan the Terrible, or Hitler are still around?

All living things are made up of cells. Some of the cells in our body die very early on in life. While still in the womb, we manufacture far too many nerve cells, and in some structures, up to 80% of them may die. This is not that they are killed off, it is a programmed death. We do not know if it is because too many of these cells are created or whether their purpose is outdated. Most of our cells continue to replicate and regenerate, although not indefinitely. Some continue to live useful lives although they do not regenerate. When they fail to regenerate adequately, signs of ageing occur, such as the wrinkling of the skin, the deterioration of the bones, the loss of a sense of smell, the thickening of the arteries. It is the death of particularly important cells, such as those that control the beating of the heart, which eventually mean the life of the whole body is extinguished.

In many other living organisms, cells continue to replicate over and over again while the conditions are right – that is the right environment and the right nutrients – and this can go on indefinitely.

These organisms, and they include sponges, bacteria and viruses, are in fact immortal. All early life consisted of these simple organisms and only a change in their environment led to their demise. In evolutionary terms, the main change came about when the sex act was introduced. It would seem that you cannot have both the joy of sex and immortality. All life that is procreated by the conjunction of a male and a female pay for it by having to die, sometimes immediately like the male octopus, or sometimes after the young have reached an age where they can look after themselves, like the female octopus, or sometimes, as with humans, sometime later. How much later is normal for humans, we do not really know, but it is conjectured that unless disease or accident intervenes, our normal lifespan could be perhaps 115 years, although as we know, one or two people have lived even longer than that.

For most of the animal kingdom, the anticipation of death is no problem, but for humans, as Descartes said, 'I think, therefore I am.'

Only by becoming conscious of one's self does one become aware of the mystery of one's birth and one's death. Although we may be aware of death, how we think about it depends in part on our age. For the young, death may appear as something glorious, sometimes eagerly anticipated. I can even remember myself as a teenager, thinking I would quite like to die young, perhaps in saving the life of another. It would be a wonderful way to die and I would be famous! Or was I afraid of what life might bring? Perhaps it is only such thoughts that have sent men willingly to war when there was no certainty that they would return. As Lucien the Greek philosopher imagines in his work 'On Grief', a son may point out the advantages of dying young because, 'he will not have to grow old, to have his father's bald head, face wrinkled, bent back and knees trembling.'

Neither will he have worries about failure, lack of money, thwarted ambition, betrayal of friends or the million other catastrophes that assault us in midlife.

Then perhaps for many young people, death is unreal, it is 'virtual', as it is in so many stories. Detective fiction would be less interesting without one or two deaths. War films are big box office, even when the hero does eventually die a glorious death. As for computer games, killing seems to be the whole point of many of them. So why does death seem to worry us as we get older? Not far from where I live, there is a 'bike run', and whenever the weather is fine at a weekend or during a public holiday, I hear the roar of motorbikes, their riders gleefully negotiating the twists and turns of a country road at great speed. This year, there are two places only 200 metres apart, where dead bunches of flowers in the hedgerow, in polythene wrappings, mark the spot where two young motorists died as a result of flying off their machines. There is no slowing down even at this point. The motor cyclists still come and still enjoy this dance with death.

The older we become; I am sure the more we become risk averse. Is it because it becomes more real or is it because we come to question more and more the purpose of existence? This is of course the basis of all religions and from earliest times there have been rituals to placate the gods, who may be responsible for all the disasters that cause death. There have probably always been rituals too in connection with the way our bodies seem to lose their normal functions and eventually decay. I did not use the word 'die', as that word has little meaning in many cultures. A body may stop breathing, but to some, the person has not yet departed. In one Malaysian tribe, they believe it takes 30 years[1]. The Pharos were not considered to have died, but they travelled to the kingdom of the gods, for which they were prepared by being provided with the objects they would need and objects that they were attached to in this world. To maintain their earthly bodies, they were preserved by mummification.

Amongst a Dyak tribe of Borneo, the dead body was handled as though it were still alive. It was kept in the house, where it had lived, sat at the table and offered food to eat. It was involved in important discussions with relatives and friends and only buried sometime later. When Europeans arrived at the village, they were appalled by this unhygienic affair, so the Dyaks compromised by building a special house for the living dead.

Even in our time and with our knowledge of science, it is not always possible to say whether a person is actually dead or not. There is a continuing dispute as to whether it is the fact that the heart has stopped beating that constitutes death or whether it is the failure of the brain to function. Very recently on a football field, a player's heart stopped beating but quick action by the medics and the ambulance team resulted in resuscitation followed eventually by a full recovery. We now have very sophisticated EEG machines, which can monitor brain activity, but sometimes it is not sophisticated enough. Newer machines are now able to detect electrical activity not just in the scalp but deep inside the brain and several people who would once have been considered dead have actually been revived after the use of this EEG scan. Perhaps the Dyaks were right to allow some time to elapse before disposing of a body.

But the story does not quite end there. Others testing out the machine discovered that it could also detect electrical activity from other machines or movement of people when there was no dead person in the room[2].

Because our sense of identity is so strong, perhaps from the very beginning of the consciousness of self, it has not possible for most to accept that death is in some way a complete and final ending. For Christians like the Egyptians, it is simply the end of one journey and the beginning of another. How we deal with the idea of death depends on our religion, our culture, our philosophy. It is a very individual and personal thing. A book by a well-known funeral director, Barry Albin Dyer[3], who did a series on TV series called *Don't Drop the Coffin* is quite hilarious (there is also the story of a friend of his who asked for the song *Fall in and Follow Me* to be played at his funeral) but he assumes that fear of death is universal. I have discovered the contrary from those of the older generation I have talked to and from what I know of those who are told for certain they have only days or months to live. Very few appear to be afraid of death itself, whatever their faith, or even if they have no faith; they are only afraid of how they will die.

Samuel Johnson was a devout Christian and during his final illness, he was much afraid of death, largely because he felt his life had been far from perfect. The fear of judgement day and the consequence of being found wanting controlled the lives of many devout Christians. The depictions of hell shown in many frescoes and paintings in Roman Catholic churches over the centuries were calculated to frighten all, into good behaviour during their lifetime. Samuel Boswell, who had dedicated himself to write a true description of Johnson, whom he considered a very great man indeed, found himself in some difficulty because he knew his idol's behaviour had not always been exemplary; in fact, it had sometimes been quite despicable.

He writes, 'His fear of death…may give occasion to injurious suspicions, as if there had been something of extraordinary criminality weighing on his conscience. On that account, therefore as well from the regard for truth which he inculcated, I am to mention (with all possible respect and delicacy, however) that his conduct, after he came to London…was not strictly virtuous, in one respect, when he was a younger man. It was known that his amorous inclinations were uncommonly strong and impetuous. He owned to many of his friends that he used to take women of the town to taverns and hear them relate their history.'

The fear of death that Johnson had had some weeks before he died are expressed most vividly in his prayers, 'Oh, LORD, let me not sink into total depravity and sin; look down upon me and rescue me at last from the captivity of sin.'

Then there came a point when he asked his doctor to tell him, plainly whether he would recover. "Give me," said he, "a direct answer."

The doctor, having first asked him if he could bear the whole truth… then declared that in his opinion that 'he could not recover without a miracle.'

"Then," said Johnson "I will take no more physic, not even my opiates."

From that time on, it would appear 'that after being in much agitation, Johnson became quite composed and continued so till his death.'[4]

He not only ceased his medication, he took very little to eat or drink for the rest of his days on earth.

The English language was Johnson's passion and he spent many, many years writing his dictionary. It is a remarkable language. Its vocabulary is so wide and so precise. Different words that appear to mean the same may have a slightly different significance, import, implication, connotation, interpretation, nuance, depending on the context.

Euthanasia comes from the Greek word meaning 'good death', but it has come to many, many things. On one hand, it could mean 'murder' when the motive for the act appears to procure some gain for those who assist in hastening death or it may be construed as 'suicide' when the dying person seeks their own death with the help of another. It can even mean 'genocide', when the Nazi regime in Germany used the theories of eugenics to justify the killing of 70,000 handicapped people in 1940. But this was not mercy killing and the people were not necessarily terminally ill.

Nazi poster from the DEUTSCHES HISTORISCHES MUSEUM that reads:

60,000 Reichsmark is the lifetime cost to the community of this genetic defective Member of the (German) race, that's your money.

When Samuel Johnson refused medication and sustenance, was it euthanasia or could it perhaps be regarded as suicide, something that would have appalled Johnson, who was a devout Christian at a time when suicide was considered a cardinal sin?

Much thought has been given in recent years to producing a hard and fast definition of euthanasia, but that helps not at all in determining how we should think about it. The problem of someone whose death is certain in the not-too-distant future and who is undergoing suffering was considered by the Greeks and by many cultures worldwide. The Jainists have a ritual called Salkehna for people approaching death when they may receive permission to forgo food. They have to be well enough to be able to make the decision themselves and they must have the agreement of their family. Their last days are spent in contemplation in the expectation of being able to attain enlightenment before they die.

Among the Eskimo tribes, where living under extreme conditions makes it inevitable that famine will strike from time to time, in the past there were various rituals that allowed older people to reduce pressure on their family by opting for premature death. Among one group, for instance, an elderly man no longer able to go out hunting with the family would stay behind and hang himself in the igloo. Before doing so, he would place a small oil lamp at the entrance to warn those returning home of what they will find. This will only happen when the family are all suffering from extreme hunger.

In this century, the problem is much more pertinent than at any time in the past because of advances in medicine means that we are able to keep people alive much longer than in the past. How many in the 19th century, when morphine could be bought over the counter at the pharmacist's, resorted to an overdose? How many doctors, even in the last century, assisted the death of a patient, unbeknown even to the closest relatives. It was 50 years before it became known that the doctor attending George V, Lord Dawson, gave him an overdose of morphine and cocaine during the night to hasten his death, seemingly so it could be announced in the Times the following morning, rather than in the working-class paper, the

Evening Standard the following evening. Was that euthanasia? Or could it even be considered murder?

Definitions of the modern idea of euthanasia usually imply a hastening of death and in certain circumstances, it may be considered acceptable. This is usually because of terrible suffering, relief from which can only be acquired in death; it is usually expected that death should be carried out with the assistance of another person; in addition, the sick person must have expressed their determination to die; and the person assisting must do so with no other motive than to carry out the wishes of the suffering person.

It is important in the 21st century to examine this most difficult of problems, because for the first time in man's history, this option will be sought by a very large number of people, people who are living longer than ever and being kept alive by medical interventions longer. To live and to die are the two most important things that happen to us. We have no control over being born, where we are born, to whom we are born, how we are born. Do we have any right to have control over our death? There is perhaps no bigger question. If you belong to a society, or a religious organisation, which because of its history, its dogma or its culture, the answer will not be decided by the individual but by the group. However, in today's western society, where such norms have often been abandoned, is it time to assert that it is the right of the individual to decide?

Very few states have recognised such a right. At present in the UK, although that right is not yet enshrined in law and theoretically euthanasia is illegal and can be considered murder, a more lenient attitude is now being taken towards it. The situation is slightly different in some other countries.

Voluntary euthanasia is legal in Colombia, Belgium, Holland and Switzerland and in at least one US State, Oregon, where physician-assisted euthanasia is legal under the Death with Dignity Act but the potential hazards for abuse are of course recognised. So, in Switzerland, the patient must take an active role in the suicide. Permitting euthanasia is fraught with dangers and there will always be in the world strange people such as Harold Shipman, whose motives will never really be understood, who was convicted of killing 15 people, but who over 25 years almost certainly killed 200 more and the figure may even run to 457.

Institutions, particularly legal institutions, are slow to change, and rightly so, but the time is now ripe for a radical rethink of attitudes towards the rights of individuals to have control over their own death. Throughout the world and throughout known history, death and belief in some superhuman power have always been linked. It has always been accompanied by ritual or dogma relating to death and how society or individuals should deal with it. Perhaps for the first time in human history, in western society, it is now possible for people to openly declare they are atheistic or who, while not denying the possibility of a superhuman being or beings, live their lives as if they did not exist, with rituals reduced to a funeral service. 'Hatch, match and dispatch' has been the only useful role of the Church of England for many people over the last century. 'Hatch' has now almost gone except for signed-up Christians; 'match' in a church is on the way out; and only death is still a church occasion for the majority, at least in Britain.

The sea of faith
Once too was at the full, around earth' shore
Like the folds of a bright garland furled,
But now I hear it no more

Matthew Arnold in his poem 'On Dover Beach' was already mourning the loss of belief back in the 19th century.

In this century, we are permitted to feel that such a faith as Matthew Arnold had is no longer essential to the smooth running of society, but what is replacing it? Religion has not only involved itself in ritual but also in the teaching of the kind of morality that makes society run smoothly. Even the simplest of societies recognised the need to have rules that curbed the natural instincts of man such aggression, selfishness, fear and anger: instincts needed for survival but when uncontrolled can lead to the breakdown of society, which is even more important for the long-term survival of the group. 'The Lord of the Flies' 5 explores this theme in a very vivid way, when a group of boys, isolated and left to their own devices on a deserted island, perpetrate unbelievable horrors. Those who allowed their aggressive instincts to take over inevitably collided with those who retained some sense of moral behaviour. For how long will it be possible in the 21st century for a society, inheriting as is does the legacy of the moral principles of Christianity, successfully to maintain secular control without the sanctions of religion?

Will then euthanasia will be considered in the light of moral principles rather than religious dogma in those countries where a particular religion is not enshrined in the constitution? This appears to be what is happening. Crucially, there have to be safeguards. If it is accepted that it is the right of the individual to decide, there has to be the assurance that their decision has been thought out over a period of time, that they are mentally capable of making that decision, that a mediator is able to ensure that no pressure has been brought to bear on the individual by parties interested in the life/ death decision and that more than one doctor has been consulted.

If the term euthanasia is accepted as applying to those terminally ill, but capable of making a rational decision, then quite different criteria need to be applied when the sick person is not in a position to make such a decision. If they have not previously expressed their wishes with regards to their treatment in what has become known as a 'living will', it must surely be important that any decision to cease treatment, to turn off life support or to cease to provide nourishment must not be left entirely in the hands of the medical profession. Not only do the nearest relatives have some right to influence the decisions, but there is also a case for suggesting that a third party – a mediator of some kind – should be involved in order to assess the motivation for the decisions made. In other words, whereas in most societies in the past, its members were jointly responsible for such decisions, because individuals cannot always be trusted to do what was right, then today we still need someone who represents society to be involved in the decision making.

All this assumes that individuals have a right to decide on the way they would like to organise their death. This is a big assumption and is at odds with most religions and with another important natural instinct. We are born as individuals, we die as individuals, but we cannot live our lives without connecting with other people.

As the 14th Dalai Lama says, "It is important to understand how much your own happiness is linked to that of others. There is no individual happiness totally independent of others."

Everything we do affects those around us, and this is especially true of the way we die. A colleague of mine attempted suicide. Fortunately, she was unsuccessful. One of her most telling comments afterwards when her friends and relatives showed how much they cared for her, was, "I did not realise how selfish I was being."

Death is your final legacy. Many have told of the amazingly peaceful and comforting experience of seeing a loved one slowly releasing their hold on life. How we die is so important to others and it explains why a coroner's verdict is so important, why years of deep sorrow, guilt and anger are experienced when a person disappears, when a death is unexplained, when a murderer goes unpunished. I remember how peaceful a neighbour of mine was in the week before she died. My words of comfort, 'You will soon feel better' were worse than banal. I totally misunderstood a situation which was new to me at the time. She said she was tired and ready to go.

'My time has come' was said with such equanimity that I was totally convinced. Such incidents shape one's own thinking in a very fundamental way. The understanding this experience gave me could only have come with such a personal contact.

For those in the extremities of suffering and pain, death is often to be welcomed, but even for elderly people for whom death is not imminent and suffering far from unbearable, in my experience, death is not feared as many people, such as Barry

Albin Dyer, the undertaker from Bermondsey believe. His experience is seldom with the dying but with the mourners to whom death inevitably seems fearsome. Bereavement is usually a far more powerful emotion than the fear of death. For most people, it is not death itself so much as the mode of dying that can produce a deep depression or sheer terror. According to Montaign, it is only the fully mature who have become reconciled to their own death, but that ignores a scientific truth, not available to Montaign – that man is born optimistic. We are wired to see the bright side of life. How else could someone like Sir James Lovelock, the author of the notion of Gaia, say, "I am 93 next year and I can look forward to the future," or Sir Tony Pratchett (aged 66), author, who says he does not want to die yet because he still wants to go on writing. He says that when that urge and ability deserts him, he may then be, 'reconciled to my own demise.'

(BBC 4 Interview).

Research done by Ajit Varki[6], a biologist at the University of California, explains this unexpected optimism and it appears to show that optimism was essential to our evolution once we developed minds that could contemplate our future. "…awareness of our own mortality would on its own have led to an evolutionary dead end. The despair would have interfered with our daily function."

I am reminded of those who have obsessive repetitive action disorder, who have to follow a strict regime of activities, such as entering a door three times or counting every metal bar in a length of railing for fear that some great tragedy would occur if the routine were not strictly followed. I know someone who has constantly to check that the photo of his son is in a particular drawer, otherwise he believes his son will die. His logical mind tells him that it is all nonsense, but he still has to do it – just in case!

Ajit goes on the say, "The only way conscious time travel could have arisen over the course of evolution is if it emerged with irrational optimism. Knowledge of death had to emerge side by side with the persistent ability to picture a bright future."

And who are the people most likely to be most optimistic? All the surveys indicate it is the over 60s, 70s and 80s. It seems that optimism declines up to the age of 40 onwards and then starts to increase steadily. That does not mean that individual old people do not sometimes become deeply depressed and suicide is not uncommon, especially among men, but that is usually when circumstances become quite overwhelming.

Have I been proposing an overoptimistic view? What of the pain and suffering we all endure from time to time; the fear of a coming operation; the indignity of being treated like a saucepan that needs a daily wash and then put back on the shelf; the pain of a terminal illness; the dread of being moved out of our home into a 'home' (what a misnomer!); the desertion by family when we really need them; all the peripheral events in our lives that promise that there is only worse to come. Are these not enough to knock the optimism out of us?

The world's great religions each give us their own answers to this. A firm Christian faith, the belief in a loving God who will always be with you can be a great support. For some, however, suffering can often make people question their belief. The Buddhist faith has a different approach inviting you to learn to accept your suffering.

Suffering begins to dissolve when we can question belief or hope that there's anywhere to hide. [7]

This requires you to learn to stop fighting against your situation and the abandonment of your anger. This is truly an answer, but it is far from easy. In all of this, perhaps it is above all necessary to have the support of people you can trust and who will reinforce your own efforts to come to terms with your suffering.

It may seem strange to those who are depressed and overwhelmed by their circumstances but many people seem to have the ability to remain positive and as they continue to face up to life's difficulties, they remain optimistic. Something about their personality or their life experiences makes this possible. A 100-year-old woman who was still active and had an amazing sense of humour spoke somewhat disparagingly of her twin sister, who had died some 30 years before, "She was only in her seventies! But no wonder, she was always miserable."

Brain scientists are now beginning to discover the difference in the brains of the optimists and the pessimists. One part of the frontal cortex (or to be precise, the rostral anterior cingulate cortex or rACC) is responsible for enhancing the flow of positive emotions to the amygdala deep inside our brains. It is apparently a failure of this process which causes depression. At present, the best the medical world can do for those suffering depression is to offer sedative drugs, some of which taken over a long period of time may cause even greater problems. New knowledge of the geography of the brain and its network of interconnections may eventually offer better help for depression, enabling our natural instinct to be optimistic to take over.

There were one or two things in common with a number of people aged 100 years and over interviewed for a BBC programme. Those who were fit, and most of them were, were all active physically, dancing, playing golf, swimming or even running a marathon. More importantly, all were taking a lively interest in the world around them, some of them still chairing meetings, visiting the local carnival celebrations or keeping contact on the internet.

As Ruskin said, "One who does not know how to die, does not know how to live."

Chapter 11 Notes

1. Medina, John J. The Clock of Ages. 1996. Cambridge University Press. Cambridge (pages 45 and 50)
2. Ibid
3. Dyer, Barry Albin. Strong Shoulders.2005. Hodder and Stoughton, London
4. Boswell, James. The Life of Johnson, Abridged and Edited by Roger Inkpen.1906. Hutchinson and Co London
5. Golding, William. Lord of the Flies. 1954. Faber and Faber. London
6. Sharot, Tali. The Optimism Bias. Journal article. Welcome Trust Centre for Neuroimaging – 2012 Published by Robinson. London
7. Föllmi, Oliver and Danielle. Offerings. Stewart, Tabori and Chang. New York. Extract by Chöndrön, Pema 17 May.

Chapter 12
Nineties Is the New Seventies

We must make good use of the life for the time we have left. This brief flash of light, like the sun appearing through the clouds.

Kulu Rinpoche

And we have so much time left! Time was when at 70 we are signalling to the world that all we wanted was to be left to wither away. Medicine, good diet, healthy exercise, an active mind and positive thinking have changed all that. To those of working age, the number of people living beyond the present age of retirement appears to be about to pose a major problem because of the need to support them economically and socially. This pales into insignificance, however, when you examine the effect that the older generation, by virtue of its numbers, is likely to have on the way society operates. This will surely bring about a cultural change of worldwide significance. The young may once again find they will need to listen to their elders. The often-quoted description of this major demographic change simply as a demographic time bomb hardly does it justice.

The graph of the Chinese population in 2009 was not the normal pyramid, with the largest cohort at the bottom, aged one to five. In this graph, each box shows the population in millions in five-year bands, those aged up to five years old at the bottom, and over 100 years old at the top. In 2009, the largest groups were aged 35 to 45 years. This skewed graph is largely the result of the one child per family policy, a policy the Chinese government felt essential, in order to control the rapidly expanding population and upon which the rest of the world looked with a mixed reaction. The Chinese government did not look far enough ahead and so they did not realise the unintended consequences; that in its simplest terms meant that at some time in the future if two people produced only one child, then that one child would have to look after two people in their old age – look after them and earn enough to help the state to support them. Then the situation became worse, because as in most developed countries, good food and good medical attention led to an increase in life expectancy. Many of the present generation of 35-year-olds in China will still be alive in 2050. As a result, the cohort of the retired, because most of the Chinese at present retire at 55, will far outnumber those of working age.

China exemplifies the modern dilemma. Everyone wants to live a long, happy and healthy life. The imbalance in the population age range might suggest society needs fewer not more old people. It is a dichotomy the world now has to resolve.

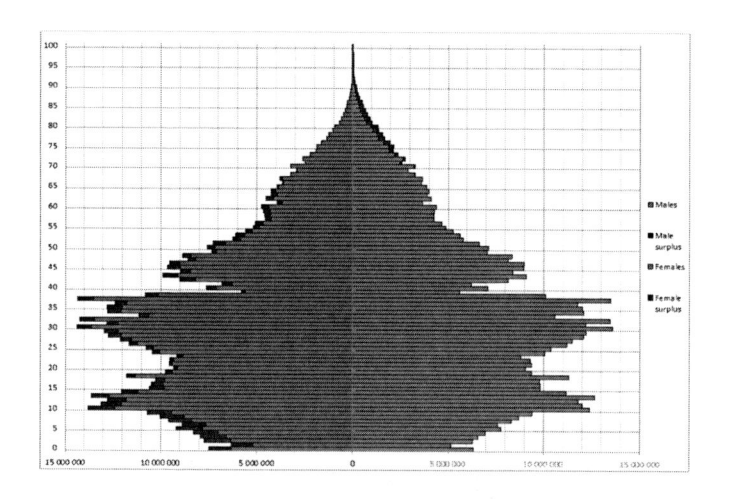

Age Distribution Graph of Population of China, 2010

It is only relatively recently that life expectancy has risen remarkably. I remember my father saying sometime before his retirement in the 1960s that his colleagues on the railway rarely survived for more than two or three years after they left work. Over the last 30 years, the life expectancy in developed countries has risen by an average of six years, in Japan from 76 to 83, in China from 67 to 73, in the UK from 74 to 80. In the developing world, the rise has been even greater; in Afghanistan from 39 to 48; and in India from 55 to 65.1 (World Bank figures).

We live longer of course because of improvements in medical science, and because in the affluent world, there is no shortage of food. We also have access to advice, some of it good and some of it quite idiotic. I read the other day that, 'Going shopping every day reduces the risk of dying by 27%'! What does that mean? Does that include Sundays, and if you only go out shopping six days a week, what then? Does it mean you are less likely to die out shopping than at home? Was it written by a desperate retailer? Are they sure it is 27% and not 25% or 28%, or even 58% or 90%? Who cares? I certainly do not intend to spend my meagre shopping money by going out seven times a week at £10 a day, instead of my present two expeditions a week, spending about £35 a time. I cannot afford the extra fares anyway.

We are living longer because we are learning the lessons of evolution that over the centuries we forgot. It has recently been discovered that it is likely that the hunter-gatherers of the Stone Age, who were nomadic, probably had a greater life expectancy than those who came after, and who established agriculture and who lived in settled communities. Not only was it necessary for our Neolithic ancestors to be physically fit to pursue their prey, but their diet, a mixture of animal products and berries and roots was a healthy diet. In other words, they ate well, they had plenty of exercise, continued to use their skills to find food and supported one another in small social groups. It was this recipe for a long and healthy life, together with the development of the brain, that allowed them to progress and to dominate the animal kingdom. In addition, they had small families as they were constantly on the move, so greater care could be afforded to their children. Later, health and life expectancy decline. In the following centuries, when people started to settle to a life dependent on permanent agriculture, they were able to have large families, and often needed them because many of the children died very young. Children are more vulnerable than adults to disease and living close together in large communities, with poor hygiene and poor disposal of waste, infectious diseases spread readily. We now know 4000 years later, why the world average lifespan became shorter than it was in the Stone Age. Now, at last, in the 21st century we have the knowledge to overcome the problems of living in towns.

With extended life expectancy, come new fears. Do young people now have visions of being debilitated for years by arthritis or cancer or spending months in and out of hospital, undergoing treatment for heart problems, or gradually being deprived of their mental capacity, subsiding into a bewildering world of non-comprehension? I guess it is a fear many people have after visiting an elderly parent in an old people's home or as they are euphemistically called today, a retirement home.

It is certainly not a new fear. Well, over 2000 years ago Plato said,[2]

'Then, undetected there steals over you in old age, into which all things pernicious and deadly in nature flow together. And if you do not hasten to give up your life as a debt due, nature, like a petty usurer, steps in and grabs her pledge – your sight, your hearing, often both. And if you hold out, she paralyses you, mutilates you and tears asunder.'

Is that how it really is? Is that what we can expect? The Roman writer Cicero[3] did not think so and what he wrote is as true today as ever it was.

Scipio to Cato: 'So far as I have been able to see, old age is never burdensome to you, though it is so vexatious to most old men that they declare it to be a load heavier than Aetna.

'I am wise because I follow nature as the best of guides and obey her as a god; and since she has fitly planned the other acts of life's drama, it is not likely that she has neglected the final act as if she were a careless playwright. And yet there had to be something final, and – as in the case of orchard fruits and crops of grain in the process of ripening which comes with time – something shrivelled, as it were, and prone to fall. But this state, the wise man should endure with resignation. For what is warring against the gods, as the giants did, other than fighting against nature?'

And Goethe[4] too knew the value of old age. His outlook was very positive. he says:

'That for which one wishes for in youth, one finds in old age.

> 'I stormed through life, through joys in endless train,
> 'Desire, fulfilment, then desire again
> 'Lordly at first, I fared, in power and speed,
> 'But now I walk with wisdom's deeper heed.
> 'Full well I know the earthly round of men,
> 'And what's beyond is barred from human ken;
> 'Fool, fool is he who blinks at clouds on high,
> 'Inventing his own image in the sky.
> 'Let him look round, feet planted firm on earth;
> 'This world will not be mute to him of worth.
> 'But now I walk with wisdom's deeper head.'

He is right! And I can say so, because I can claim to be old myself, but you do not have to believe me! One day, you will find out for yourself. I am not claiming that I am actually wiser, but I have found you really do look at the world in a different way when you are old – in a way that appears perhaps mysterious and quirky and not altogether agreeable to younger people.

As Baroness Bakewell said of the House of Lords, "Do bear in mind that these old goats have lived lives of enormous scholarship and expertise. They have a body of wisdom that has to be utilised." It is quite important though to know which old goats to listen to.

There is one obvious difference in our attitude. I cannot be really excited about the news that we might get a high-speed rail link between London and Scotland, sometime in the future, when I am not likely to be here to make use of it. For perhaps the first time in your life, you know for certain that there will soon be a time when you – that unique individual that has seen so many things, done so many things, had so many memories – will just disappear. For some of course, this is almost unbearable, and they search for the everlasting life, preferably here, but if not here, in some paradise somewhere else. So, what matters to you is no longer the future, but it is the present – the people around you, the people with whom you are in daily contact, and of course, your family. That does not mean you are not interested in the daily news; for many old people listening to or watching the news, becomes almost addictive – something that becomes part of their daily timetable. Routine becomes vitally important, the more so if you live on your own.

As someone said, 'When you are old, the days pass slowly, but the years fly by.'

A daily routine helps. It could also be that the news makes you feel connected to the rest of the world. My friends certainly like to be in touch with world news far more than ever most of them did when they were younger.

It is not, however, the things that you take an interest in that might change. It is much more fundamental. It is a changed outlook on life. I am just reading an hilarious fictional story called, 'The 100-year-old man who ran away (in his slippers!) and disappeared'5. The title says it all: not only is it a précis of what is in the book but also because it shows the different outlook of the older person. You no longer bother too much about what people think about you. It is too late for that. So, telling this story you do not need to think up a short really clever witty title to impress people with your brainpower; you just tell it as it is.

The book is hilarious because of the common-sense attitude of the characters, not exactly devoid of emotion, but approaching the world with impeccable logic and detachment. So, when you read about a villain with a case full of illegal money who finds himself in a freezer and then discovers, what to him is an incredible fact – that he has no signal for his phone – the reader does not become particularly distressed to learn that he is frozen to death during the night because someone forgot to turn off the freezer. You are not even particularly saddened to discover that later his body is hidden in a container that will soon be on its way to Ghana. After all, he was a rogue and even his rogue of a boss thought he was stupid, and all seemed to agree that the world was probably a better off place without him. When his robber co-worker slips up on elephant poo and then gets sat on by the elephant commanded by our 100-year-old to 'sit!', the only possible response to this poor man's death is laughter.

This emotional detachment from how people will look at them, which allows older people to speak their minds with few reservations, may not be always acceptable to those younger, who really do not want to listen to the wise words that some old people have to offer or conversely the constant moaning of others, about the 'good old days', the depravity of the young, the decline of civilisation. Yet, even the moaners and groaners may offer grains of wisdom for those intelligent enough to sift them out. The freedom you feel to speak out in this way when you are old is an unexpected bonus.

There is the story told by Diana Athill[6], of Alice Herz-Sommer who at the age of 103, said, "Life is beautiful, extremely beautiful. And when you are old, you appreciate that more. When you are older, you think, remember, you care, and you appreciate. You are thankful for everything."

For everything? The amazing thing about this quote is that it came from someone whose life was full of sorrow. She was a Jewish woman born in Czechoslovakia who was destined to become a famous pianist. She was quite brilliant, studying under a pupil of Listz, but her dreams were shattered in 1939 when Hitler invaded Czechoslovakia. She was never to be a world-famous performer. Instead, she was sent off with her husband and her son to a concentration camp at Theresienstadt. She survived the war, as did her son, but her husband was moved to Auschwitz and she never saw him again. We do not know what other horrors and tragedies she witnessed but we know that returning home to Prague, there was nothing left for her there – no home, no family and no friends. She and her son decided to go to Israel, where he became a well-known cellist. Eventually, she came to England with her son and lived independently in a tiny flat in north London. Her son died at the relatively early age of 65. She lived through her music and played her beloved piano every day for up to three hours. She also went swimming every day until she was 97 and lived her life joyfully in a genuine state of forgiveness. She was able to say, 'You are thankful for everything.'

It is unlikely that everyone would be able to say that given her life story. She would say, "I hate no one. Hatred only brings more hatred."

She died in February 2014, aged 110, having said in an interview, "I think I am in my last days, but it doesn't matter. I have had such a beautiful life. And love is beautiful. Everything we experience is a gift, a present we should cherish and pass on to those we love."

There must have been something special about her genes or her upbringing to give her such a positive outlook on life. We are all so very different and for that reason I believe there cannot be just one solution for how society should deal with its older people. We all have different pasts and different needs in the present.

Recently, there was a television series which explored this particular theme in a programme in which four celebrities stayed for four days with different elderly people to look at the problems they face and to examine how their lives could be made better.

Alan (not his real name) was a well-known reporter who had spent his life reporting world shaking-events from on the spot. He stayed with a lady called Polly who lived on her own in a small cottage in a village. Although not quite a recluse, she appeared reluctant to mix with the villagers, who could not understand her aloof attitude and gossiped about her because she never took part in communal activities. The word 'cantankerous' seemed to sum her up, so she was left alone. Meeting her, Alan's first impression was that she appeared to be quite happy living on her own without any social life. She had a regular and rigid routine and watched television quite a lot. The programme she never failed to watch was wrestling on a Saturday afternoon. Although to Alan, whose life had brought him excitement on a daily basis, her life seemed boring in the extreme and somehow purposeless. She appeared to be quite content, wanting nothing, least of all, wanting friends or change.

The only person she appeared to have had any regard for in her whole life was her father, who was buried in the local churchyard. Visits to the churchyard were her most important outings. Both her parents had been very strict, and she had had little love from her mother as a child. Who knows how this had shaped her life? She had a motto. Did she acquire it from her father? It was 'Give up or get on!' and presumably that was how she had managed to carry on after her father died. She had been able to accept the limitation of her life and appears never to have had the opportunity of making friends.

As Alan said, "Polly is who she is," and he realises there is no point in trying to change her. She was very grateful for the company of Alan, who could empathise because although his mother was loving, he had lost that love aged six, when she died. No one ever replaced her. His solution to accommodating himself to that loss had been to create a phantom mother to convince the children at school he was no different to them. Polly's mother was all too real.

If Polly has had any thoughts about her future, and surely she will have had, perhaps she hoped she one day she might have a heart attack and that would be the end. Days or even weeks later, someone might notice that she had not been seen about the village and the awful truth would be revealed.

She had died alone, and no one knew. The feeling of sadness would be cloaked perhaps by a feeling of communal guilt. Why had they not known? Why had no one noticed? I am reminded of the sick joke, 'My neighbour is very well looked after, judging by the number of milk bottles on her doorstep.' It is, however, difficult to feel anyone was to blame, when someone like Polly clearly wanted to be left alone.

If not a heart attack, perhaps she might develop a debilitating illness that would make it difficult for her to look after herself. Alan's attempts to get her out to meet people were not very successful. Transporting her to a residential home would be like sending her to a torture chamber, and the word 'torture' is not too strong. At first, she might resist it with all the energy she could find, but finally she would succumb, eventually dying alone and forgotten. In an ideal world, the answer would be to have someone as sympathetic as Alan in daily contact with her in her own home.

But where would such a person come from? How would they be paid for? Another elderly lady who featured in the programme lived some distance from her daughter, who had no idea that her mother was trying to feed herself on £3 a week. The well-paid celebrity who went to live with her for a few days was challenged to do the same. It was clear that clever buying was not the answer to this problem. It needed someone from outside to look at the real cause of the problem, an experienced outsider she could trust; in this case, a celebrity being paid to feature in a TV programme. The answer lay in looking for cheaper accommodation, closer to her daughter's home, and that allowed more money to be spent on food.

The story illustrates how there is often need for advice and both moral and practical support from someone independent of the family. In another peep into the secret lives of others, the TV visitor was able to discern that the real, deep-seated love between a bedridden husband and his devoted wife had been eroded by misunderstanding because of the exhaustion of the woman and the fear of the man that she would desert him, sending him off to live in a home. It took an outsider to bring them back to understanding one another again so that the husband was prepared to go into respite care while his wife went on a cruise to renew her strength, returning to care for him.

These brief glimpses through the windows of the lives of the elderly illustrate how different are the circumstances, how different are the needs and how different are the solutions. We are all individuals. Even identical twins will develop in different ways as they interact with the problems that life throws their way. By the time we reach old age, how differently we have been shaped. Once when I was at my school assembly, I suddenly became obsessed with looking at peoples' noses. They still interest me, and it is fascinating to see how as people get older, their shape, to me at least, appears to become more and more individual, more and more prominent. That may just be a whim, but I think there is no doubt that old people develop a marked individuality, with unique qualities, unique approaches to life and certainly they are unique in their needs. It would seem obvious then that a caring society should find a number of different ways of providing for old age as a result of forethought and planning, rather than with the ad hoc solutions, which seems to be the way society deals with it now.

Chapter 12 Notes

1. World Bank figures
2. Plato – Axiochos 376b Quoted in Chap 2 History of Old Age.
3. Cicero Senectute
4. Goethe Faust, Part! Act V, trans Philip Wayne Page 27 Ibid
5. Jona Jonasson and Rod Bradbury? TiptreeBook Service 2012
6. Diana Athill 'Somewhere towards the end' page 173

Opening quotation: Kulu Rinpoche, 30 January to be found in Buddhist Offerings 365 Days Oliver & Danielle Föllmili published by Stewart, Tabori and Chang, New York, Thames & Hudson (no publication date given).

Chapter 13
Modern Society – Help or Hindrance?

The girls of this school have assisted in the preparation of hampers for needy pensioners, making them cakes, etc. Six recipients died during the year.

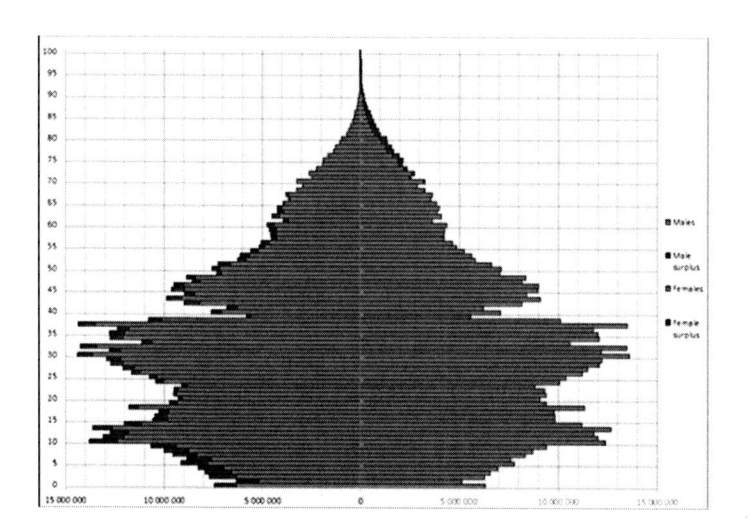

Providing support for people for whom old age has brought unexpected and unprepared for problems need not always be a question of money, and it is the newly retired and fit who when organised can provide one solution. Interesting experiments along these lines are already taking place, particularly in Denmark, in the USA and now in Britain.

In Rotherfield in Sussex, a country village of some 3,000 residents, support for the elderly comes from a community organisation which arranges whatever help is seen to be needed, from transport to changing light bulbs, from digging gardens to writing letters, from counselling to computer tuition.

This morning, I found myself trying to deal with something that I found impossible, despite trying what I considered were ingenious solutions. I simply needed to take a heavy old television set upstairs. I thought of using a plank. Then I got a two-wheeled trolley, but it was too narrow to support such a wide object. I thought of encasing it in a sheet and dragging it up the stairs, but I guessed the material would not be strong enough. So there the large TV sits at the bottom of the stairs and I am hoping someone might come by, today, tomorrow or next week, who is strong enough to lift it. The Rotherfield St Martin Community organisation sounds like just the answer.

Although such organisations do not offer full-time care, they can provide regular support. Falls in the home become increasingly a problem for many, with loss of balance, poor eyesight and arthritic limbs. Last week, a friend of mine fell in the sitting room of her small bungalow and it took an unbelievable hour and a half before she could find a way of getting back onto her feet. A daily knock on the door from a community volunteer is all that is needed if there is no neighbour to make a regular check.

An hilarious example of the unexpected occurred when a friend of mine came to stay in my house to look after my dog while I was away. On my return, I immediately looked for her and called out to her, but there was no response. Perhaps she had gone for a walk. I unpacked the car and then began to look for her in earnest. I stood at the bottom of the stairs.

"Pamela! Pamela!" I shouted. This time there was a response.

A small squeaky voice called out, "Help! Help!"

Rushing upstairs, I traced the sound to the bathroom. There was my friend, laying in the bath fully clothed, head against the taps.

"What?" I began to shout.

She interrupted me, "Get me out of here! I can't get out!"

It seems that after having a bath, she just could not pull herself to a standing position. She had managed to empty the bath, then leaning over the side, she had grabbed some of her clothes, then she lay there, waiting for me to come home. I was shocked and wondered what would have happened if she had had that bath a day or two before I was due to return. My friend – she just laughed! The only way I could think of absolving myself from the guilt of it happening again in the future was to go out and buy an attachment for pulling yourself out of the bath.

Such volunteer systems as the Rotherfield St Martin Community are unlikely to be adopted universally and they depend crucially on a willing and capable organiser with vision. Nevertheless, perhaps they could become more widespread with financial and administrative support from the government. They are not only cost effective in the help they give but the scheme also gives meaning to the lives of retired people willing to offer their services.

It is now well established that it is from the elderly that the largest number of volunteers are recruited. This applies not only in the voluntary sector but in the public sector too. A large proportion of those who make up our local councils has always been from among the retired. It is only in recent years that our leading politicians as well as our prime ministers have been relatively young. John Major was the only man in the 20th century to become Prime Minister while still in his 40s. Churchill took over leadership in the Second World War at the age of 66 and most were over 60 when they took the prime minister's office.

In the 21st century, prime ministers have taken up office in their 40s. What do they do when the lose their job? There is now an increasing reservoir of experienced people who retire early from business or politics who no longer require to earn their living and who are prepared to volunteer their talents for the service of the community. I have seen this in action in my local community, which, although still a working community, also has a large number of retired residents. It is a small town of some 3,000 people, where for years, the parish council did its duty, dealing with the occasional problem of dog fouling or holes in the road. Its most dramatic activity came about as a result of the district council paying a considerable sum to upgrade the attraction of the town for tourists by laying down cobbles in the main street. There was outrage! Any change was bad change, even if it meant changing back to what it had been a 100 years ago. And who wants tourists, anyway?

The parish council won and the district council had to bear the cost not only of laying down the cobbles, but of taking them up again.

That was 20 years ago when the Parish Council consisted of local people (i.e., people whose ancestors had lived in the town), a council whose composition rarely changed year by year. That is no longer so and many of the present councillors, though by no means all, are people who have spent their working lives elsewhere. Now retired, they are taking up the challenge of bringing a dying community back to life.

Booktown status has been established, there is an active twinning organisation, there is now a town plan, a community building has been purchased, a community owned charity shop supports local initiatives with finance and now there is a plan to rebuild the community hall. Nearly all these initiatives have been led by so-called 'incomers', mainly retired or semi-retired with not only valuable skills to offer but more importantly leadership.

This pattern is being repeated in rural or semi-rural locations all over the country and must be set to increase. The challenge will be to see this happening in urban communities, where housing patterns often segment communities, grouping together those of similar income. Nevertheless, once the number of retired people reach a critical mass, it is possible to imagine that voluntary groups will begin to use their talents to improve services in their area.

The fact is, so many people now retire with ambitions, with energy, with expertise and with the desire to still have something to live for, perhaps wanting to leave a legacy as important as or more important than the legacy of their working life. There are very wealthy businesspeople now giving their time and their money to international charities. There are professional people anxious to take on new challenges. I have been associated with buildings restoration committees, made up entirely of retirees, who take on the restoration of valuable historic buildings that no commercial operator would look at; of others who have started up sustainability projects, building wind farms or hydroelectric schemes too small, too risky and too time consuming to be undertaken as a business project. Headed up by people who are not only committed to achieving something valuable for the community before they finally take to the wheelchair (or even after they have taken to a wheelchair), these people often have greater motivation than those merely doing a paid job. They also have a wealth of experience to bring to the project. While it is usual for artists, musicians, actors and writers, as well as farmers, fishermen and self-employed odd job men, whose life is their work, to continue working for as long as they are fit enough to do so, often into their 80s and 90s, it is now becoming usual for those whose lives have been spent in less rewarding work to undertake something of significance to them and to the community in their retirement.

There is a sign that the tilt in the age demographic towards older people who have time and money may be beginning to overcome our ingrained western culture, that has emphasised that is the duty of the individual to provide for himself and his family (and in the past, it was always the man, of course, who took on that responsibility.) This is in contrast to communal societies, where the responsibility is shared by the group.

The attitude has changed slowly over the last 200 years, when people began to realise that it was not enough to leave the care of the needy to charitable institutions, such as church organisations. They had insufficient resources. The discontented poor were seen as a threat and so the state started to take responsibility for caring for them in institutions, such as the workhouse, the asylum or the hospital. Responsibility for looking after the poor in society was taken away from the family and the local community and passed to the state. In a society where there was such a huge gap between the rich and the poor, this was the answer. In the late 19th century, when there were men and women of sufficient means to dedicate their lives to improving society, they led the way in education, helping the elderly and infirm, in caring for orphans, creating great museums and art galleries. Now, this work is being shared by the state and to an ever-greater extent, by the large numbers of fit retired people, who may not be wealthy but who no longer need to rely on paid employment. They become the trustees of retirement homes, of charities to research diseases and support the sufferers, cutting the costs of administration and bringing their lifetime's skills to raising money through charitable channels.

When I first visited the USA, I was struck by the lack of fences or hedges around individual houses. At the front, there was more often than not no boundary marking at all. At the sides and the rear, any fence was usually low and open. It was such a contrast to the high brick walls that separated the rear yards of urban properties in Britain, even when the houses were part of a terrace. Upper-class Georgian terraces, of which Downing Street seen regularly on TV, is a good example, are still nearly always fronted by iron railings guarding an area a metre or two wide. It may be interesting to note that during the Second World War, people overcame this desire for a strong barrier around their property and people accepted they had to give up their iron railings for the war effort. The feeling that 'we are all in it together' did not survive and by the end of the 20th century, we had a prime minister who could announce that 'there was no such thing as society.'

The attitude still persists that everyone's home is their castle, surrounded by a boundary barrier and a firmly shut gate. How postmen must hate opening and shutting gates! Is this a continuing sign of our belief in our right to set ourselves apart from other families? It is only in some working-class neighbourhoods, in some small villages or on some islands in Britain that people do think more of their homes as open to the community and where their doors are never locked. This depends of course on trust, of knowing your neighbours and of behaving as a good neighbour, something that broke down with urbanisation and perhaps with the development of suburbia. In urban areas, old people may often have lived for some years at a distance from their families, and they remain isolated. Even among the wealthy, there is often an expectation from the family that they are better off excluded from the community (such as it is) once they can no longer look after themselves: and so they are hived off into a 'home.'

This failure of integration in society has led to the latest infection – ageism. Saga undertook an online survey of their readers in 2010. While not a representative sample of the country as a whole – not many of our inner-city population will be going on Saga cruises or buying the walk-in baths advertised in their magazine – nevertheless, it shows up some concerns common to all those who are retired. Problems of money of come high on the list of gripes, but unsurprisingly, ageism in all its forms came top of the list; ageism at work;

ageism in the media; ageism in politics; ageism in recreation; and ageism in the National Health Service.

In the NHS, which now has old people to treat than at any other time, it is unforgivable that the structure of hospital care, the training of nurses, the management systems and the spending on research have not yet caught up with the new type of care that its patient population needs. The ageing timebomb has not yet been recognised! Maybe it is simply a wilful blindness, which shuts out the fear of what it will mean when there are more old people than young or is it because it is now the young who make all the decisions? Those in the survey demanded more old people in parliament and particularly in senior positions, which seems strange to those of us who always thought of most politicians as being old men.

Management in government or in commerce is now a career in itself. You no longer work your way through any organisation. You get your degrees and your qualifications, and you go in straight into management.

Qualifications are now the key to success, not ability, not dedication, not emotional fitness, not inspiration, not interpersonal skills, not even honesty or standards of morality. Young people's talents are invaluable, but the balance needs redressing, and that will involve reversing the cultural change that has come about in the last 50 years. It will not be easy.

The Saga survey also showed the need for a more flexible approach to the retirement age. As the cost of pensions to the individual and to the country increases, this is one change that is perhaps inevitable. When economic necessity coincides with a social need, changes come about. In China, the age of retirement was 55 years, simply because grandchildren who continued to live in the town where their parents were born needed grandparents to look after them when both their parents started to work hundreds of miles from their hometown. I guess the retirement age in China may now move upwards as the one and only child faces the prospect of finding the wherewithal to look after two retired parents.

This was a point taken up by Joan Bakewell, one of eleven well-known personalities that Saga asked for their opinion on what needs to be done. What she clearly recognises is that the role that older people can play in their workplace must be appropriate to the skills that their age can bring. They may no longer have the flare and energy needed for management, but their experience and skills can be put to good use passing on skills, in mentoring or for example or in reviewing policies in light of the success or failure of previous initiatives. The work needs no longer be full time and the flexibility of that could be a bonus to a company that needed more help at busy times. This will require not only that employers recognise the value of their older staff, but that those whom we might call the semi-retired, are themselves prepared to adapt to a smaller, but no less valuable role in the workplace.

She concludes, "The sooner we look on the bright side and recognise there will be gains for everyone, the happier our community will be."[7]

Of the comments from the 11 personalities writing for Saga, four others, Julia Neuberger (social reformer), Tom Wright (CEO at Age UK), George Magnus (economist and author) and Katherine Whitehorn (writer) all chose the need to allow people to go on working longer as the most pressing issue.

Examination of cultures in the past and cultures in the present in other parts of the world can open up new perspectives on how the older section of the population can fit in. Yet, it is a different world we live in, a world that is ever more affluent, ever more urban. For the first time in history, urban dwellers exceed those living in rural areas. It is a world that will contain an ever-increasing proportion of old people, both those who are active and those who are needing constant care by others.

The world has changed but man himself has probably changed little since homo sapiens came down out of trees and started to walk on two legs and to develop a bigger brain. His physical attributes are largely the same and his emotional needs have probably not altered. The ageing process still shows up in the wrinkling of the skin, the deterioration of the senses, the loss of some functions of the brain and the greater proclivity to disease. Yet, as so many societies have recognised that old have a unique and highly valuable contribution to make to society. The length of time for the development of an infant into becoming a fully capable adult is much greater in humans than for most other animals and the number of years adults live beyond the age of child begetting is also exceptionally long. It has been suggested that the latter developed because of the need for grandparents to assist with child rearing when the parents were fully occupied with providing food, clothing and shelter. Humans have evolved in a way that requires the elders to support the life of the family. In addition, the old have a unique and highly valuable contribution to make to society because of their wisdom, their experience and their freedom from the stress of providing for the family. It is a pity we use modern terms such as 'pensioners' or 'senior citizens', instead of the entirely appropriate term of 'elders.'

Perhaps this provides the clue as to what is the greatest change that has come about in western society, especially in the UK, and the one that explains why there is little understanding between the old and the young. It is the lack of contact. We no longer live in all-age communities. Perhaps one of the most chilling incidents I heard about was from a lady living in a middle-class suburb, in a small house built in the last 20 years, over 80 years old, but still driving a car and walking the beach, with a house that was immaculate and an interest in photography and computers.

Her immediate neighbour said to her one day, without any explanation, "You shouldn't be living round here you know; you don't fit in. It's time you were in a home!"

The British have almost the worst reputation for the way they treat the elderly in Europe. Out of 20 countries studied, they are 17th out of 20 for the percentage of the national income spent on care and help for pensioners.

The physical split between the generations, with the geographical separation of families and the social separation, means that youngsters do not join bridge clubs or play bowls and old people do not attend youth clubs, which, by their very name, keep out those beyond a certain age. There are so few social occasions, or social venues, unless you count the supermarkets, where people of all ages meet up or bump into each other. If there was money in it, perhaps supermarkets would cash in on this.

Meanwhile we live with the world as it is, and it is not all bad. Who would not want to stay in bed all morning if they felt like it? Who would not want to have time to engage in a thrilling new hobby? Who would not want to 'go out in my slippers in the rain' and never worry about what people will think about it? Who would not want to shout 'rubbish' at the television set when there is no one there to chide them? Who would not want to hear their granddaughter whisper, 'I love you Granny?'

Retirement now is often the beginning of a new life that may well last 25 or 30 years; a life when remarriage is not unusual – my own grandmother remarried for the third time aged 82. I never had the courage to ask her about her sex life in old age, although I know she enjoyed it in her younger days. But I wondered! In an Age UK survey of the over 65s, almost a quarter of the respondents said that age had not affected their sex life and one in eight declared that they would quite like to find new ways of priming the excitement of the sex act, an act which encapsulates the intensity of 'being', heightened because you join in that sense of euphoria with another.

For passion is not the prerogative of the young. Passion creates an intense awareness of self, of what life means to the 'I' and the most passionate are those who want to get every ounce of experience out of living because of the imminence of death. It is those who have a life-threatening illness who create a 'wish list.'

OK, there are times when the limbs ache, when you have too many pills to take, when you fear the next trip to the doctor, when food no longer tastes good, when you miss all the best bits of the conversation because you forgot to put on your hearing aid ('What are they laughing at?').

Then you are free to say with an explosive growl, "Old age is a bugger," but you do not really mean it. You just enjoy using language you would not have dared to use in your youth. Perhaps it is only those who are facing the imminence of death who are really able to live in the fullest sense of the word. It is the old who can ponder the beauty of the world around them, living in the moment as they watch a blackbird flying off to its nest with a worm in its mouth, or see a tulip in the jar on the table drop a petal.

This is universal not only amongst all people now living but al who have ever lived. It was the philosopher Montaign, who in the 16th century pondered on death and came to the conclusion that not only was death nothing to be afraid of, 'but it should be pondered and confronted because it is the key to living.'

He also said, "I want death to find me planting my cabbages, neither worrying about it or the unfinished gardening."

Montaign had not always felt like this, but his father, younger brother and best friend had all died within a short time of each other. Only one of his five daughters lived to maturity and he himself nearly died in a horse-riding accident. He became delirious and vomited blood, but he survived, and it completely changed aged his attitude to life – and to death. His legacy was his writing, which even today gives insight and hope to many.

Not only great men but everyone has something to offer even in their last days – the smile or the grip of a hand from someone on a sick bed that inspires belief in man's humanity and so often shows that a serene acceptance that death itself is quite normal and is part of the beauty of life. The silent wisdom of the dying is more penetrating and potent than the noisy wisdom of those still in the fullness of life. And the dying know that their reward for good or ill is that they will live in the children of the future.

I do not worry about death, but I do worry about my legacy. What my children insisted on writing on the gravestone of my husband were the words, 'He lives on in all of us', and how true that is whether you are talking of friends or descendants. My husband lived a quiet life, content with his garden and his pipe of tobacco but people still remind me of his idiosyncrasies, his jokes, his amiability. He never aspired to money or power and left no landmarks, but what he was, lives on among his friends and his attitude to life lives on in his children.

Richard Holloway, the ex-Bishop of Edinburgh, memorably wrote:

Our brief finitude is but a beautiful spark in the vast darkness of space. So, we should live the fleeting day with passion and, when the night comes, depart from it with grace.

Epitaph

To the memory of Mrs Pirns, who passed away September 10th. Peace at last. From all her neighbours of Princes Avenue.

(Leicester Mercury)

The meaning of life is that it stops.

Kafka

He died in life, yet in his death he lives.

From an elegy to a friend by Master John Bowhay.

Death is the most liberating answer of how to live a life. It makes it possible to do just that: live.

Montaigne